T0285511

UNLOCK YOUR LEADERSHIP STORY

UNLOCK YOUR LEADERSHIP STORY

How to Build Understanding
and Motivate Teams

Using Fables *and* Folktales

PAT WADORS

WILEY

Published by John Wiley & Sons, Inc., Hoboken, New Jersey.
Published simultaneously in Canada.

For general information on our other products and services or for technical support, please contact our Customer Care Department within the United States at (800) 762-2974, outside the United States at (317) 572-3993 or fax (317) 572-4002.

Wiley also publishes its books in a variety of electronic formats. Some content that appears in print may not be available in electronic formats. For more information about Wiley products, visit our web site at www.wiley.com.

Library of Congress Cataloging-in-Publication Data is available:

ISBN: 9781394264469 (cloth)
ISBN: 9781394264476 (ePub)
ISBN: 9781394264483 (ePDF)

COVER DESIGN: PAUL MCCARTHY
COVER ART: © GETTY IMAGES | JOHN LUND
AUTHOR PHOTO: COURTESY OF THE AUTHOR

SKY10086282_092724

I dedicate this book to my family. To my husband, Dave, for teaching me to dream bigger and believing in me every step of the way. To my amazing kids, Ben, Eddie, and Katie, and our growing family: Nicole, Lauren, Everly and Emmett. Your love and encouragement mean everything.

Contents

Contents

Prologue

I'm so excited that you are reading or listening to this book! The audience—you—are why this book came to be. I didn't want to write about my profession or about a company. Instead, I wanted to serve you and support you on your life's path. Who couldn't use a helping hand? In fact, if I can help one person discover their superpowers, build confidence, and be inspired to strive to live their best life—then I have fulfilled my purpose. To achieve that purpose and to unlock your potential, I will share wisdom, tips and insights gained throughout my personal journey—both the highs and lows. But the magic—and lessons—truly come together through the insights from fables and folktales. The moral lessons of these stories are incredible—standing the test of time. They are a quick reminder to me, and now hopefully you, to live life to its fullest.

I'm also thrilled to write. Who knew? When I was approached by the publisher, I wasn't quite sure about writing a book, how I would fit that work into my schedule, and if the book I did want to write would be of value. It's not that I don't love to tell a good story, because I do, but writing a book seemed out of reach. Both the idea of sharing something that is personal so publicly and having the grit to write a whole book that others found of value was a bit overwhelming to even contemplate.

Once decided, I jumped into this adventure. I didn't realize how much fun this project was going to be until I started. It flowed. The stories made me laugh and some made me cry. They came easily and with such clarity. When asked why it was flowing, the only answer I had was that this book has been in development for decades, because I have been living these stories, learning the lessons, and sharing them along the way.

Finding My Courage to Write

I am both introverted and dyslexic. I also have a bit of imposter syndrome. Self-doubt sits on my shoulder—we are close friends. (Although I have learned how to brush it off my shoulder from time to time!) The combination of these traits strikes me as I sit down this morning and write this book, especially because my dyslexia worsens when I get anxious, like a stutter. And believe me, I'm anxious (and excited!). Without this spell check, half of my words would be misspelled by now!

But because you are reading this book, that "out-of-reach" goal is now real. I just had to change the story in my head, get that imposter off my shoulder, and find my courage, or rather remind myself of my purpose. And let's not forget a few wonderful nudges along the way moved things along faster than I anticipated.

The Two Nudges

I guess I needed a lot of encouragement!

August 27, 2014—Nudge 1

Once upon a time, when I was the head of human resources at LinkedIn back in early August 2014, I was participating in a leadership offsite with our top 200 global leaders. This was a two-day event packed full of social networking, presentations, training, and facilitation. Everyone was grouped in tables of eight coworkers—many we just met that week. Basically, it was an event that would exhaust me and every other introvert if we didn't carefully watch our energy.

I was "managing" my energy carefully throughout the day. I found myself once more standing in the back of the room while someone else held the audience's attention on a key topic. My chair toward the front was empty. Near me were my fellow introverts, leaning back against the wall or near the door. We gave each other the nod, basically saying, "I see you and I understand! Save your energy. You will have to talk soon."

While I was standing in the back of the room, one of our leaders, Steve Johnson, walked up to me and asked me why I was not in the front of the room taking more of a leadership role at that moment. I informed Steve that I was an introvert and took this moment as a break—to not be "on"—and to build up my energy for the hours ahead. He was surprised. He didn't see me as an introvert. I explained that he primarily sees me when I am "giving my energy" to the employees or to our customers. When I can take a step back and breathe, I take it! Being a leader demands that I be heard and visible, while also navigating the use of my energy so I do not get exhausted.

Steve is extroverted and led our user experience design team. He was so good at networking and bringing energy all the time! In our brief conversation, he asked me to speak to his team as he believed 30–40% of them were in fact introverts. He was curious if I had tips or tricks to help engage fellow introverts. Steve was unclear about how to best lead them and to coach them in their careers. Then he quickly pivoted and stated that I MUST WRITE about my experiences—in fact, publish a LinkedIn blog post. He wanted me to share that you can be a successful leader as an introvert. Immediately, I said no. I was happy to chat with the team, but not willing to write about it.

I had never written anything publicly to date. Nothing.

The very idea of writing something and sharing it with the world to be available for judging or grading made me anxious and afraid. I repeated my answer—NO—but that I would be more than willing to chat with the team. However, Steve did not let up because he believed that others would benefit from my journey.

Each day for the next five days Steve "nudged" me; even texting me on the weekend. Finally, on Sunday, I sat down and wrote my story. I wrote it the way it flowed through my head. I wasn't an expert on introversion versus extroversion. But I did have my lived experiences. I wasn't sure that what worked for me would work for others. But just maybe it could. If that happened, then I would be manifesting my purpose:

I need to leave the world better than I found it.
To be kind. To give more than I get. To make a
difference.

—My purpose statement written
on a whiteboard

Reminding myself "to give more than I get" changed my mind. I thought that if I shared my experiences, it just might help someone else navigate their path in a better way and give them courage to achieve their goals in life. It was that belief that gave me courage to write.

That Sunday afternoon I completed my first long post. I read my article several times, but I just couldn't push the publish button. I was scared. The "imposter" sat stubbornly on my shoulder once again. There was no way to push her off! The next day I reread my article, striving to find the confidence to post, and then I reminded myself that it is not about me but more about helping others.

Finally, I shared my article with someone on my team. They found value. That was enough of a push. My article was published on Monday morning, August 27, 2014. Due to nerves, my hand was shaking when I pressed publish. After that moment, I called Steve and informed him of the post. He was happy—I was scared. *Now what?*

What I didn't realize, or even dream was possible— was that my life and therefore my personal story would be changed from that single act. I just didn't know how fast.

October 23, 2014—Nudge 2

Fast forward only two months later, when I was kicking off LinkedIn's annual Talent Connect conference. An amazing memory moment, when the vibrant lights, new smells, and energizing sounds can still be brought into clarity in my mind. That day I was asked to introduce Arianna Huffington on stage at our conference. Approximately 8,000 attendees were waiting to hear Arianna talk about her journey to health, embracing sleep, and combating burnout. I was a major fangirl and loved the way she told stories.

In preparation for Arianna's introduction, I was expected to meet her for the first time in the green room a few minutes before our segment. (The green room is where we had our VIP speakers get ready for their presentations.) When that time came, I remember being led through this dark passage behind the stage by one of the stage managers carrying a flashlight. The sound technicians were getting ready for the next speaker, running their tests. No one paid me any attention. I finally entered the green room, my smile a mile wide. In my head I was wondering how best to introduce myself and express my excitement for this moment. Then something unexpected happened.

Arianna turned around when I entered. She looked me in my eyes, reached for my hand, and said:

> "Pat, it is a pleasure to meet you. I love your work! My daughter is also an introvert, and we loved your post. Please continue writing. You made a difference. Thank you for sharing your story."

I don't think I said anything right away. I was too busy talking to myself in my head.

> *Wow! She knew me? She read my post? Is she sure it was me? Her daughter read it and found value in it? It mattered!!*

I was blown away. I must have mumbled something, but I could not tell you what I said. She asked if I knew Susan Cain, the author of *Quiet*. Of course, I saw Susan's TED Talk and had read her book! Arianna insisted that we should meet. She felt our stories together would be wonderful.

After the conference, she immediately introduced Susan to me. Susan and I got to know each other and collaborated, further helping me on my journey to better leverage my introverted superpowers. But that's another story for another time.

Confident and Now Courageous

I was committed from that point forward to sharing my stories. To seek to learn, to share, and to elevate others. To be vulnerable. The imposter sitting on my shoulder still visits but is easier to knock off. This book—about 10 years later—is a manifestation of that belief in self that was sparked by that first LinkedIn article and inflamed with Arianna's supporting comments.

Thank you, Steve, for pushing me! Thank you, Arianna, for your encouragement. My life and my ability to pursue my personal purpose is better because of you and those "micro moments" of encouragement.

Your Invitation to Embrace the Challenges Ahead

Now, back to this book you are reading. My hope is to encourage you as the author of your destiny to intentionally design your future self and manifest the desired moral of your story. Together, we will explore the power of storytelling throughout human history and share stories that hopefully shape your understanding of the world and yourself.

You have choices coming your way, and you may be wondering: what's next in this book? What fables are coming, and why? In the pages ahead, I assist you in your quest to craft your personal leadership story. Your reading journey will start with these elements:

The magic and power of storytelling with key insights in Chapter 1. The magical impact of storytelling in our brains helps unlock what is within you. Simplicity and clear moral lessons are why I love fables and folktales as a key tool to coaching!

Next, you will dive into four different chapters that help you define the magic elements of your quest, determining your desired destination. You will touch an elephant to gain perspective, chat with Goldilocks to find just the right fit, and engage with the three little pigs as they brave the wolf and set their goals—to name a few.

After that, you will meet the emperor, the crow, a frog, and finally Mulan. One of these stories has been around for 1,600 years! They are your wizened guides to assist you in your quest. Because what is a quest without challenges and a merry group of travelers to assist you? Each guide offers insights and wisdom to help you achieve your goals.

And finally, at the end, you will find your guided journal to begin your journey. To design your quest. The story of YOU.

Please continue with me on this adventure. You may want to skip around and find your own path, but be aware that each chapter builds on the prior one. Each chapter shares a moral lesson or two. The fables, personal stories, and tools shared in this book were created to inspire, motivate, and drive positive change for you and those around you. To unlock your leadership story!

I'm excited about the possibilities that lie ahead. Let's go!

Chapter 1

Stories Unlock Your Superpowers

"Do not follow where the path may lead. Go instead where there is no path and leave a trail."
—Ralph Waldo Emerson

Bedtime stories told to me by my dad, dinner table storytelling with friends and family, family gatherings at holidays with everyone talking at once updating everyone on their latest adventures, Nancy Drew mystery books read at the Jersey Shore, and Sunday night Disney movies. These are my cherished memories. I might not remember every part of those stories, but I remembered how they made me feel.

I am the youngest of eight children from an Irish Catholic family—growing up listening to stories. Stories that made me laugh and some that made me cry. I learned a lot about my family's history, learned not to be afraid of thunder and lightning, why telling the truth was important, and the value of hard work—all through stories. Each story shared by parents, siblings, and grandparents resonated with each of my siblings differently—each one of us taking away a different lesson or, rather, the "moral of the story." That is normal. You interpret what you hear based on your own experiences, challenges, and desires.

Although I loved the Nancy Drew Mystery series, I fell in love with a good dramatic story thanks to Nanny, my grandmother. My grandmother was an amazing storyteller. Nanny traveled the world, had wonderful adventures (many I'm sure she exaggerated), was married several times (one husband was an Antarctic explorer in 1933!), and had a single child—my mom. Nanny stayed with us often. I loved her. We all did.

She was magical. Nanny would light up a room when she began to share stories of the family, her travels, her mishaps, and memories of our childhood that we loved listening to—especially at bedtime when we wanted to stay up late! She told stories with humor, humility, and with a flair for drama. While she would tell her story, she would wave her arms and her tone of voice would change, almost as if she were telling us a secret. Then she would look us in the eyes and pause, right before the climatic ending. We were all held in suspense. It didn't matter if we had fought throughout the day or the fact that we had up to a 15-year age gap between us, we were all bound alike by her story. Her stories built a sense of family, history, and connection. They gave us joy. Her laughter was contagious.

Storytellers are magical.

When I was at LinkedIn as their chief human resources leader, I was asked by Jeff Weiner, our CEO at the time, "What do you stand for? What is your statement?" He was seeking a single sentence—a tagline. After a few conversations, I told him "I don't have a single statement. I tell stories." I realized then that this was my tagline!! I tell stories. (Thank you, Nanny!) This is how I have connected with others and continue to learn—both in the telling of stories and in listening to other people's stories. Your stories.

The Power of Storytelling

Although I have loved stories since I was young, I didn't understand the true power of storytelling until much later in life. Stories have the power to change the world—and YOU.

In 2016, when I was exploring the power of belonging, I learned the true magic of storytelling, specifically personal stories. It was storytelling that was the best tool in the toolbox to create a sense of belonging. Not only did others' stories of belonging, or in fact when they did not belong, create shared learning but it also created a vulnerability that created a deeper sense of social connection between individuals who shared their stories.

In my personal research, I learned about the neuroscience behind the feelings you have when told a compelling, personal story. When you hear a story from the beginning, middle, and then the end, you release chemicals in your brain, which pull you into that story. You see yourself in that story. It is that magical element for all of us in which we get to learn from each other and begin to see each other's perspective in a clearer light. Besides helping us learn, these chemicals also helped manifest empathy and compassion. Stories are amazing!

We Are Pulled Toward Stories

Research says that we are driven to belong. Our brains are genetically hardwired to motivate us toward connection and belonging—it's how we survived and thrived for generations. In the early days of humankind, by belonging to a tribe, you would be safe, share food, and have a community around you. This need to belong, our social needs in fact, are managed by the same neural networks as our primary survival needs such as food and water. Think about how hungry you get at the end of a day! That is such a compelling feeling.

Belonging is a compelling force at work, too. The pull to belong is so strong that some people do not share their authentic self at work—they cover parts of themselves

Stories Unlock Your Superpowers

from others to fit in. To appear like they belong. This act of covering takes a lot of energy, so if a company can create moments of belonging, embrace a culture of belonging and inclusion, they will outperform their competitors. Leaders that tap into this—by creating a sense of belonging on their teams—exceed their goals and reduce attrition.

Greg Walton, a professor of psychology at Stanford University, showed that belonging and attachment to a group of coworkers is a better motivator for some employees than money. His research, which originally focused on university students, also showed that mitigating threats to a sense of belonging helps people significantly reduce stress levels, consequently improving physical health, emotional well-being, and performance. Therefore, creating a wide sense of belonging can become a competitive advantage for any company and a healthier life.

Unfortunately, the sense of not belonging is widespread, yet few people openly express that feeling. We think we're the only ones who feel that we don't fit in; in reality, it's a very common feeling.[1]

My personal belief, or rather my experience, is that bridging that sense of not fitting in gets harder as we age. Think about how quickly small children make friends on the playground. Now in my late 50s, I see how many in my peer group, if they didn't already establish a social circle, struggle to find their "tribe" and make new close friends. That was my case, too. When I moved to a new city in 2020, it took me several years to get to where I am just now feeling like I belong. I had to demonstrate more personal courage—especially as an introvert—to reach out to folks I met and see if they wanted to be friends. Do you want to take a walk with me? Meet for coffee? Not every encounter resulted in a new friend, but I got more comfortable sharing that I wanted to make more friendships. That was new for me. It was the pull to belong that gently pushed me forward to friendships.

Now you know that you and I both want and need to belong. We want to be our authentic selves and thrive. But how? What is the best tool to create a path to belonging? To grow as individuals? To survive and thrive in this world? A story.

Stories Facilitate Belonging

Stories can be used to accomplish the following:

- *Increase understanding:* Stories provide you with a concrete example of how an issue affects people's lives.
- *Build empathy:* Stories can help you experience the world through the eyes of another person. They help build connections and share learnings.
- *Drive action:* Stories show you that change is possible. You see how others have tackled life's challenges and thrived.

The Brain Science Behind the Story

The secret behind this power is our brain, in our genetic code. How amazing. We are genetically wired to react to a story whether told orally and in written form. It is because of this reaction that stories have been captivating humanity for centuries—and me for decades! It turns out that storytelling triggers a cascade of neural activity that makes us feel, learn, and remember. So many times, I can hear a story and know exactly where I was when I first heard it. How it made me feel. Fun fact: songs can create a similar effect!

Our Brains Mirror

When we listen to or read a story, our brains begin to mirror the speaker or writer's experience. We create synchronization of neural activity. As we follow along with the story, our brains fire in the same patterns, enabling us to create a shared mental representation of the unfolding events. The details in a story heighten this shared mental representation. This mirroring is another reason why smiles and laughter are contagious!

Our Brains Create a Bond

Stories also trigger the release of oxytocin. This has to be one of my favorite hormones in our body. This neurotransmitter is often associated with love and bonding. Oxytocin promotes feelings of empathy, trust, and cooperation, making us more receptive to the story's message and more likely to connect with the characters. This is a big component to building a sense of belonging and psychological safety. It promotes positive social behaviors.

Our Brains Trigger Excitement

As we anticipate the story's resolution, our brains release dopamine, a neurotransmitter associated with pleasure and reward. This dopamine surge keeps us engaged and motivated to continue listening or reading, ensuring that we don't miss out on the story's conclusion.

Storytelling is not just a form of entertainment, it's a deeply embedded human instinct that taps into the very core of our brains.

Storytelling is as old as humanity itself! It's through storytelling that we have survived and thrived.

Our earliest ancestors used cave paintings and other forms of visual art to tell stories about their lives and experiences. They warned of dangers and showed celebrations. These stories were passed down from generation to generation through oral tradition. We learned not to go into the dark woods because there was danger in that direction. We learned to tell the truth so that when we really needed help, others would believe us and come to our rescue.

The Evolution of Storytelling

Stories were shared orally for generations. Then the invention of the printing press in the fifteenth century revolutionized storytelling. For the first time, books could be produced quickly and cheaply, making them available to a much larger audience. This invention led to a surge in the popularity of storytelling. In the centuries since the invention of the printing press, storytelling has continued to evolve. New forms of storytelling, such as film, television, and digital media have emerged (TikTok being a recent phenomenon that is based purely on short story videos format), and these forms have become increasingly popular.

I love fables especially, because they are short stories and always have a moral lesson. As a human resources leader, I've leaned on fables and folktales to coach and guide my employees, mentees, and even my children. The stories created a shared understanding that made it easier to address a behavior, values, challenges, or desired outcome we were striving to achieve. It was a great shortcut to address the nuance of any given situation.

What I also love is that fables typically feature animal characters. Who doesn't love an elephant? Or see the humor in a lion and a mouse becoming friends? Because they are so relatable, fables have been around for centuries.

One of the most important figures in the history of fables is the French fabulist Jean de La Fontaine. Published in the seventeenth century, his work is known for its humor and social commentary. His most famous fable is "The Raven and the Fox." The fox's flattery led to the raven's downfall. This story offers a timeless message about the dangers of deceit and the importance of being cautious, discerning, and critical in our interactions with others.

When I've been asked to coach or mentor someone, I typically start with a story. I also ask them what their story is—what is their origin story and where do they wish to go in their life or in their career. These stories unlock opportunities, create trust, and encourage mutual understanding.

In Summary: Embracing Your Stories

I encourage you to embrace the stories that are coming your way in this book! I've shared stories from my lived experiences and stories shared by friends, family, and coworkers—all of which are intended to leave nuggets of wisdom for you. All of which are anchored with a fable or a folktale. The wisdom shared as moral lessons will help guide you on how to interpret the world, inspire you to perhaps modify how you lead others, and hopefully provide you with the confidence to navigate your life's adventures and all the challenges ahead.

> Fun fact: Did you know that the word *moral* comes from the Latin word *mores*, for "habits"? By learning from fables, you can create healthy habits for a well-lived life.

Now it's time to go on this journey together. Thankfully, we are not alone. Together with our fable friends, like a warrior and a frog, you will emerge stronger than how you entered this adventure. Skip around or go in sequence—it is your adventure to take. Once you have finished with the fables and folktales, you will discover a working guide to assist you on your personal journey.

As Ralph Waldo Emerson said, *"Do not follow where the path may lead. Go instead where there is no path and leave a trail."* May this quote inspire you to forge your own path and create something new.

Note

1. Pat Wadors, "Diversity Efforts Fall Short Unless Employees Feel That They Belong," *Harvard Business Review*, https://hbr.org/2016/08/diversity-efforts-fall-short-unless-employees-feel-that-they-belong.

The Elephant and the Blind Men

Evolving Your Perspective

*I*n a village, there lived six blind men who had never encountered an elephant. One day, an elephant was brought to the village, and the men became curious to understand what it was like. Unable to see, they decided to explore by touching different parts of the elephant's body.

- The first man touched the elephant's side and described it as "smooth and wide, like a wall."

- The second touched the leg and felt its massive form, calling it "tall and sturdy, like a tree."

- The third reached for the trunk and surprised by its flexibility, declared it "like a big snake."

- The fourth grasped the tusk and felt that it was sharp and pointed, describing it "as a spear."

- The fifth felt the ear and found it large and flat, saying it was "like a fan."

- The last man touched the tail and perceived its thinness, concluding it was "like a rope."

Each man, based on their limited experience, had formed a completely different understanding of the elephant. When they later shared their descriptions, there was confusion and an argument as each insisted that they were right. None of them could comprehend the whole picture based on their single point of contact.

Suddenly, a wise man passing by noticed the commotion and inquired about the situation. Upon hearing their conflicting descriptions, he chuckled and explained that each man had experienced only a part of the elephant, leading to their unique but incomplete understanding. He then described the entire elephant, highlighting the different

The Elephant and the Blind Men

features they had individually touched, and revealed to them the true nature of the majestic creature.

Perspective Is Everything

I start with this fable of the elephant because perspective is everything. I invite you, the reader, to broaden your perspective of self, others, and where your possible future adventures might take you as you read this book. If you keep your mind open, lean in with curiosity, and invite others on your journey, magic will unfold.

But where did this fable come from? The story of "The Elephant and the Blind Men" is a classic Indian fable told in various cultures with slightly different details. The version I shared is the most widely known. I tell it often. Each time I share this story, it is a gentle reminder to me to take off my blinders. To open my eyes wider and see the bigger picture.

The first time I heard this story referenced at work was at Applied Materials. I was new to operations, having left my HR role to learn new skills. Basically, I was in a steep learning curve and wanted to absorb information/wisdom quickly! In one quarterly business review, a senior executive asked our team to share our hypothesis on why we were having such difficulty with a key large customer. Our installations were failing. They were taking too long, we wasted extra materials, and we were losing trust with the customer.

Each team member shared their unique perspective on the issue based primarily on their functional view. The materials lead spoke about poor product specifications, so they shipped wrong materials. The electrical engineer team lead spoke about the poor quality of insight into the install base configuration data. In other words, each member was limited in their view from the beginning. In fact, after six members spoke, the leader declared, "All of you are right and all of you are also wrong."

I was not the only one in the room confused by this statement. He shared that it was the classic "seeing the trees but not the forest." And then he proceeded to share "The Elephant and the Blind Men" story to further drive home his point. You see, each of us saw the problem from our functional expertise. We did not look at the whole ecosystem. I was fascinated. To solve the whole problem they had to depend on each other, as there were several connected issues to address.

We stepped back to see the whole "elephant." We asked each other to clarify questions regarding their recommendations. As that discussion continued, our energy went up, we got smarter and more confident that we could solve this issue—quickly and without wasting extra materials. Our leader agreed. After we implemented our solutions, that sense of achievement and our ability to work more cohesively together made us an even higher-performing team. We also increased our trust in each other. Touching the elephant became our mantra for success!

Fast forward to when I was the chief human resources officer at ServiceNow in 2017. Along with John Donahoe, our CEO, the senior leadership team created what we called our *social contract* with each other. We were a new team composed of leaders who had been with the company a long time and about a third of us were new to the company. We needed to build a new team and build trust. The social contract was a way to move that ball forward with intentionality.

In our social contract, we listed behaviors that we would hold each other accountable toward to enable us to be an extraordinary, healthy leadership team. One of those tenets was inspired by this elephant story. We agreed to the following: *We will argue like we are right but listen like we are wrong.*

The primary purpose of this tenet was for us to do our homework, form an opinion, and then, once raised, actively listen to each other's perspective with humility. To be open to the idea that our ideas could be wrong or incomplete. That there may be more than one way to approach a problem. This tenet made us stronger and smarter.

Thank you, elephant! I will continue to take this lesson forward in my career and my life.

My Story: Perspective as a Parent

I have discovered that finding the "right" perspective on all things is key. It has never truly been easy for me, as I tend to spin in my head, especially late at night, worrying about something or someone. I fixate on the issues as I see them. My husband says I go into a rabbit hole like *Alice in Wonderland*. Getting a broader perspective is healthier, so when I spin, I reach out for guidance and hopefully learn to broaden my perspective in a healthier way.

As a parent, my pediatrician was a key source for a healthy perspective in caring for our kids. She gave me the confidence I needed. When our three kids were young, between six and nine years old, they were busy with sports and school. I continued to work full-time and struggled balancing everything. There never was a week that went smoothly. The biggest struggle was finding ways to give them a balanced healthy meal, and I could forget about a consistent dinner time or dinner as a family around a kitchen table! The guilt was bad. McDonald's chicken nuggets was our "go-to." I dreamt of my children turning into nuggets in my sleep!

Well, it was that dreaded annual pediatrician visit. I loved our doctor, but I was embarrassed that I wasn't a great parent. I was ready to confess. I trusted Dr. Pitts-Davis, but she was also direct in her feedback. She had been on this journey with us since my kids were born. As soon as she walked into the room, I confessed right away to all of my bad parenting traits. Fast food, inconsistent mealtimes and bedtimes. Not sure they even brushed their teeth at times. (Thankfully they still have all of their teeth!)

Dr. Pitts-Davis just calmly looked me in the eye and asked a few questions (helping me touch the whole elephant):

- Do your kids eat a vegetable once a week? I said yes. We love broccoli!

- Do your kids eat protein weekly? Again, I said yes. Don't chicken nuggets count? Hotdogs? And that occasional hamburger we cooked on the weekends.

- Do your kids eat fruit weekly? My answer—most weeks. Oranges were hit on the ball field!

- Do your kids eat cereal in the morning or some break-fast meal? My answer—most days!

- And are your kids happy, active, and making friends? YES! Maybe too active some days for us . . .

(continued)

The Elephant and the Blind Men

(continued)

Dr. Pitts-Davis then declared I was a great parent. Or at least one that was not doing harm. I was normal. We were normal as a family. She gave me a perspective that I needed. Each day can flex. Don't stress. That perspective was liberating! I don't have to be a perfect parent each day. I learned to take a more balanced, longer-term view—both of myself as a working mom and in how my kids were growing into healthy young adults.

In reflection, I was just seeing the trunk of that virtual elephant. I only saw that I was not giving my kids that healthy meal every day and perceived that others were able to do what I could not. It was the one area I fixated on as I felt I could not meet my own expectations of a mom, wife, or employee. With the help of Dr. Pitts-Davis, I saw the whole elephant. And it was a healthy thriving one, too.

Reflection: Gathering Your Story Elements

This book in fact is about pulling together various parts of the "elephant" for you to begin and or polish the person or leader you want to be. Without a broader perspective, it is extremely challenging to be the leader you want to be—you will miss critical parts that might have an outsized negative impact on those around you.

For me, I had to learn and evolve who I am based on feedback and a ton of self-reflection. Self-reflection is not easy! I saw and continue to see things that I can improve. Many times, I get in my own way. But to be my best version,

Unlock Your Leadership Story

I have to "touch the whole elephant" of who I am and who I want to become when I "grow up." When I go too fast, my bad habits can sneak back in. That is why reflection at regular intervals is key.

Reflection—in an honest way—can be hard. All of us will see things that are not exactly great. To truly know where you want to go—how you want to live your best life—you need to see both the good and the bad. I had to find the space and courage to do just that, and I strive to do it often. (Things—bad habits—do sneak up on me every now and then!) When I began my journey, I wanted to know how my story will end. How it could end if I took more ownership for the journey and the options ahead. To do this exercise, begin by asking yourself the following questions:

- What is your desired legacy?
- What elements do you want to see in yourself?
- Why do you want to change? And why?
- Will you be committed to the work to modify negative behaviors when needed?

To do this process, I needed to get feedback from people I trusted to start seeing the whole me and see the parts that I wanted to reshape. I prioritized the areas that I was willing to work on to be better. And as I have evolved, I continue to seek feedback and to hone the person I want to become. As a result, the spinning in my head has decreased. And I am more content, happier with who I am each day.

(continued)

The Elephant and the Blind Men

(continued)

What About You?

You also have many facets, but do you know all of them? Which parts of yourself do you share with others? Who gets to see the whole you? How would your friends describe you? Your neighbors? Your coworkers? Do you like what they see? What elements would you like to change? Or which trait do you want to make even bolder?

Now here comes another tricky part—truly seeing your team, family, and friends. How clearly do you see others around you? Do you have biases? Do you see them only in a single setting? Or do you see them in various locations—at home, at work, or at the store? How consistently do they behave in these different settings?

With the data that you observe, can you see the whole elephant? When someone at work acts out differently, do you see the whole picture? If not, do you seek to understand more? Or in reverse, when you change your behavior pattern, do you give those around context into why?

Sometimes, we only get a glimpse of something, like the tip of an iceberg. There is so much below the surface! We need to find a way to see below the water line. Curiosity, good listening, and care will help you see the whole elephant.

In Summary: Striving to See the Whole Elephant

- *Strive to understand all perspectives:* Each blind man, touching only a single part of the elephant, forms a unique but incomplete understanding of the whole.

Likewise, your individual perspectives are limited by your experiences and access to information. You should be open to different viewpoints and try to piece together a complete picture before forming conclusions.

- *Communicate and collaborate:* When the blind men share their individual perceptions, they gain a fuller understanding of the elephant. This emphasizes the importance of communication and collaboration. Through open communication and sharing unique perspectives, people can collectively approach a more complete and accurate understanding.

- *Beware of subjectivity and bias:* Each blind man interprets their experience based on their own prior knowledge and biases. Be aware of your own subjectivity and potential biases when interpreting information. You should strive to be objective and consider different perspectives before making judgments.

- *Truth is relative:* No single blind man possesses the complete truth about the elephant. This highlights the relative nature of truth. Each perspective holds a fragment of reality, but the complete picture emerges through diverse viewpoints and understanding the limitations of each individual perspective.

- *Accept, understand, and respect:* Ultimately, the fable encourages acceptance and respect for diverse perspectives, even if they seem incomplete or different from your own. Each viewpoint contributes to collective understanding, and recognizing these limitations fosters cooperation and a more nuanced understanding of the world.

Remember, we will argue like we are right but listen like we are wrong.

I encourage you to see the "elephant" that is within this book. Each fable, folktale, or personal story is meant to guide you on your quest and broaden your perspective. To help you see the whole you and the potential within you. These stories will help you determine your quest—your destination—as well as how you want to navigate your journey toward that destination.

However, like the blind men touching the elephant, these stories and lessons reflect my perspective and are shaped by my bias and my experiences. You have traveled your own path in life, so you might also see different lessons from your lived experiences. Please "touch the elephant"—read the chapters—where instead of more blind men, you will get the chance to meet a crow, a frog, and a courageous warrior, to name a few. Reflect on their insights, pull out your own insights, and strive to incorporate the nuggets that help you on your path. Whichever path you take!

But most of all—enjoy the ride! Life is meant to be lived to its fullest, and I hope you find joy and comfort in the stories ahead.

Chapter 3

Goldilocks and the Three Bears
Finding the Right Fit

*O*nce upon a time, in a small cottage in the forest, there lived a family of three bears: Papa Bear, Mama Bear, and Baby Bear.

As usual, each morning the bears prepared their porridge. Papa Bear cooked a large bowl of his thick, hearty porridge, Mama Bear prepared a medium-sized bowl of her flavorful porridge, and Baby Bear stirred up a small bowl of his sweet porridge. This time, however, the porridge was a bit too hot. Leaving the porridge to cool, the bears set off for a walk in the nearby woods. They left their door open for a cool breeze.

Meanwhile, a young girl named Goldilocks, with her curious nature, was wandering through the forest. She loved to explore! After a while, lost and hungry, she stumbled upon the bears' cottage. Intrigued by the inviting aroma, she stepped through the open door.

Discovering the three bowls of porridge on the table, Goldilocks couldn't resist the temptation. She tasted Papa Bear's porridge, but it was still too hot. She tried Mama Bear's porridge, but it was a bit too spicy. Finally, she sampled Baby Bear's porridge, and it was just right. She ate it all up, leaving the bowl empty.

Feeling tired, Goldilocks decided to rest. She tried Papa Bear's chair, but it was too hard. She tried Mama Bear's chair, but it was too soft. Finally, she settled into Baby Bear's chair, and it was just right. She curled up and fell fast asleep. (In some versions of this story Goldilocks goes on to try out their beds for her nap, finally falling asleep in Baby Bear's bed.)

After their walk, the bears returned home, ready for their porridge and rest. Papa Bear discovered his porridge *bowl had been moved a bit, Mama Bear found her chair out of place, and Baby Bear was shocked to see his porridge gone and his chair occupied by a sleeping girl!*

Goldilocks awoke to the surprised groans of the bears. She realized her intrusion and quickly jumped up, accidentally breaking the little chair. Frightened, she ran out of the cottage and back into the forest. Later, after a bit of reflection, Goldilocks came back and apologized for her behavior to the bears. They accepted her apology and they became friends forever more.

My Goldilocks Story

I love this story for so many reasons! Although I don't condone entering someone's home uninvited—or eating their food without permission—I do love the lessons threaded throughout this story. The two biggest ones are the lesson of self-discovery to figure out what works for you and the power of curiosity.

This story came to mind when I was in college, as I tended to relate most of life's lessons to the moral of the story found in fables. It was a simple and relatable way for me to express myself when I wasn't sure exactly what to say. The moral lessons also inspired me along my path.

In this chapter, I will share my journey of self-discovery, along with some wisdom I've gained along the way, and introduce you to the Goldilocks framework. This framework was created by me to assist not only myself but also others in becoming the leaders and creators of their future, rather than being led or overly influenced by others' expectations. May these stories and framework help you find your "just right fit."

Finding My Right Fit

At age 18, a freshman in college lost in a sea of expectations, I followed my brother's path to Louisiana Tech, which was a constant uphill battle academically. I felt like this was the supposed-to route, not mine. It was there that I began to lean into finding my "right fit."

To avoid pursuing college degrees that focused on subjects that were difficult for me and to lean on something that I loved doing, I initially majored in fine art. It was a special program at Louisiana Tech that was given to only a few of the applicants. I've loved art since I took my first art lesson at age seven from a neighbor. Art is my passion, and it was my go-to throughout high school when I struggled with math, science, and spelling. Art in any form gives me confidence and joy. Unfortunately, although I had some talent, I discovered that I didn't have the commercial motivation to pursue this as a career. I discovered that challenge in my very first semester (thankfully, I learned this quickly!)—at my first art show.

At the end of the semester, I had completed several pieces for an art show to showcase my skills and hopefully sell a piece. It was at that show that I discovered something within myself. This show wasn't just about the transactions; it was about connection. I wouldn't part with my work to someone who didn't get it, even for a fat price tag. Conversely, a genuine connection, a spark of understanding that transcended even my own perception of the piece, ignited joy that transcended money. The result? Not a single sale. No money exchanged hands! Five of my pieces were given away to kindred spirits, and I was very happy with that outcome. They were wonderful people who left happy. However, my dad did not. He was worried about how I would make a living.

This love of creating and giving continues to this day, a silent language that connects me to loved ones and those in need. These creative, connecting moments still fill my soul. I am glad I kept the pursuit and the gift of art in this fashion.

During my second semester of college, I pivoted and majored in psychology. Because I loved getting to know people and learning why we behave the way we do, I thought this would be a great major to pursue. I wanted to help people improve their lives. I was motivated to solve problems. People's problems. In my first week that semester, at my first class for Introduction to Psychology, our professor outlined the course and the primary role of a psychologist. We were instructed to help guide the person to self-discovery so that they could in fact fix their own problems. We could not tell them directly how to do it. We had no control over any actions they took to strive to improve their lives. I wanted to solve problems and do it fast. I wanted to do this at scale. Another lesson learned; this chair didn't fit me either.

After that second semester, I was faced with a life-changing moment. In March 1983, my mom passed away. She had been sick for several years, but still her passing had a profound impact on me. Between her death and learning that being either a commercial artist or a psychologist wasn't a fit for me, I increased my focus into discovering my true fit and my purpose.

Life shifted. I moved back home and transferred to Louisiana State University (LSU) in Shreveport so I could be close to my dad. It was time for both of us to start anew. For me, my first step was to go to the career center at LSU to meet with a guidance counselor. I needed help. Part of me just wanted her to tell me what to do. But a bigger part of me wanted something bigger. Something that got me excited. I just didn't know what that was going to be—yet.

Finally Being Diagnosed (and Seen!)

The career counselor had me fill out forms and write about things that I loved as well as areas that I was not interested in at that time. When I was done with the forms, she asked me, "Pat, how do you navigate your disability?" What?? What disability? I looked down at my body and didn't see what I thought she saw.

She then began to highlight my misspelled words that were in the documents I had completed for the evaluation. Once again, I felt the familiar shame that I had in so many of my classes when I was being graded. I started to withdraw into myself, but then she explained that she believed I was dyslexic. *I had never heard of that disability before that day*. She outlined my symptoms and shared how she believed my brain was processing. She shared that being dyslexic doesn't affect my IQ. I was elated! This was the first time I had a word, a description that represented my struggles. It freed me from labels that others had ascribed to me for years. It also opened a world of possibilities as I did not see this as a weakness. She explained that with the emergence of computing power, spell check and so on, I could accomplish anything. It was just a matter of finding what I was passionate about. I believed her and then I began the journey of believing in myself.

When I shared that discovery with my father and my uncle, both had a similar reaction. They wanted me to hide the fact I was dyslexic. That future potential employers would see that as a weakness. I followed their advice for about a decade. The cost of hiding that part of me was great. As a manager, I later realized that everyone learns and grows differently. It wasn't until my mid-thirties that I had the courage to share my diagnosis. In fact, by then I considered it a superpower and wanted to share my learnings with others.

Even though I became comfortable sharing my disability, it wasn't until very recently that I learned my IQ score. I had avoided IQ assessments for decades, but I needed to participate in an executive development evaluation that included an IQ test. Maybe I hesitated taking this test earlier, as I wanted to believe the counselor that being dyslexic did not equate to a lower IQ and that this belief in self was enough. It definitely was enough for me all of those years.

Finding Human Resources

It was also in that counseling session that she shared that the results of my assessment could lead me toward teaching, social work, or human resources (HR) (called *personnel* at the time). They all felt like potential fits, but HR sounded most interesting to me. After that session, I researched the profession, interviewing my dad and his twin brother, Uncle Roland—who were both in HR. What they shared got me excited. I could help people and companies solve their problems. I could have a positive impact on culture and employees. I found my spot. My calling. It just felt right.

Not only did I love that career path but I also knew that I wanted to become head of HR one day. I wanted to align all of the various job functions within HR to best serve the company and their employees. To move or focus on different components to drive higher outcomes. The impact to the business could be amazing if done well! My uncle described that on average, 80% of a company's operational expense is the cost of talent. So, if a company wanted to win in the market, be able to recruit top talent, and retain and develop that talent, they would need a strong head of HR. There were many career paths that could lead to that role, but I was sure I wanted to shoot for that top role. I wanted to help build a high-performing, healthy company at scale. This role in any company, would be the key to achieving that objective.

My path became a bit clearer. I knew then that I needed an education and to develop new skills to achieve my goal. What I didn't have at the time was clarity on my immediate path. Once again, I was unsure on the what, when, and the how. What educational path would fit me? Where in HR should I start? I was afraid of making the wrong career moves. Do I just take on the roles that others ask me to do, or should I have my own opinion? At that time, women did not typically have the top job. I was continuously guided to be in benefits or recruiting. No one suggested the top role. Not even my uncle or dad.

Along came Goldilocks into my head.

She was curious. She had a desire. Goldilocks, to fulfill her curiosity and achieve her desired goal, tried the various porridges, chairs, and perhaps even their beds. She was fearless. She figured out what fit her. She didn't have a singular path. Her adventure, curiosity, and spirit sparked my imagination.

Like her, I came to realize that it was the journey of discovery that was a part of the goal. Learning what you like and what you do not like were equally important both in my personal life and my career. I was ready. I "entered the cottage," so to speak, to begin my adventure. Soon thereafter I moved to New York by myself at age 20 and transferred to Ramapo College in Mahwah, New Jersey, where they offered a special program to approximately a dozen students as a pilot to support careers in personnel. This was before degrees in HR were available. This modified program was perfect for me. I pursued my BS degree in business administration with a minor in psychology. I kept the psychology pursuit, because, after all, this role still helps people solve people's challenges.

Pivoting for Experience

After graduation, my uncle continued to mentor me. With his guidance, and channeling my inner Goldilocks, I spent my first decade of my career learning, rotating into various functions within HR, as well as transitioning to different industries. I was hungry to learn and did not want to get pigeonholed into a single career path or industry. Optionality was my goal. During that journey, I built skills, gathered some wisdom, and figured out a couple of my superpowers. I made mistakes and learned from them. I spent time being a compensation analyst at Viacom, facing head-on my anxiety about how my dyslexia could affect my performance. At Medco, I became a technical recruiter and then rotated into employee relations. These roles pushed me and my introverted style to connect with employees and be more visible. After Merk acquired Medco, I pivoted again to go into sales as an account manager to learn more about the business. This rotation gave me butterflies for the steep learning curve, but it also strengthened my confidence in my ability to learn. To build relationships based on trust.

Essentially, each pivot (porridge, chair, or bed) that I made enabled me to discover new skills, gave me confidence, and provided many lessons that I needed to learn to get to the next destination on my journey. These pivots, and the ability to pivot into whole new domains, became the foundation of my technical skills, my overall confidence, as well as enhancing my business acumen for being a chief human resources officer.

Lessons Learned from Goldilocks

Although Goldilocks, metaphorically, has been with me on my journey of discovery, I think the first time I referenced that Goldilocks' analogy as it relates to career mapping was at Applied. At Applied, it was very common for leaders to tap someone on the shoulder and assign them a new role or project. When this occurred to me, I was concerned about the "career detour." Would that project help me achieve my long-term goals? Build new skills? Or were they just leveraging strengths I had already developed? I loved being exposed to new challenges, figuring out what worked and didn't work for me. However, I wanted to also be in the driver's seat as it related to that journey.

It was then that I felt the urge to get a coach and lead my future. Like Goldilocks, I was curious to truly get to know me, my skills, passions, and development areas. I am grateful for that moment of enlightenment and the courage to pursue my "just right" fit.

I continue to lean on Goldilocks and the moral of her story to this day:

- *Finding your fit is a journey, not a destination:* I hear Goldilocks in my head as she keeps prompting me to explore, giving me insights from which to spring from. These insights guide me to be better, stronger, and wiser. As I age, I can see the shifts in my thinking. In addition to channeling my inner Goldilocks, I use this fable and the moral of her story when guiding others to discern their own career path and life choices.

- *Goldilocks needed structure:* Inspired by Goldilocks, and responding to my mentees who wanted a tool to leverage in their pursuit of the right fit, I crafted a Goldilocks framework. It was the codification of my thoughts and the coaching that I received. This tool and approach continue to assist me and others in our pursuit of self-discovery and decision-making. What I realized, when using this tool, is that it is actually harder than it appears.

- *Knowing oneself is hard:* To truly sit in self-reflection and to be truthful to oneself is a challenge. We need to take the time. There are elements I found within me that I loved, and other elements that I didn't quite like to own up to. Sitting in self-reflection enables me see when I need to change and shift. Sometimes it is shifting a mindset, other times it is humbling to realize I do not see myself as clearly as I need to in order to be the best version of me.

Interested in self-discovery? Want a personal adventure? The next section explores the Goldilocks mindset in action.

Finding Your "Just Right" Fit: The Goldilocks Framework

I crafted the following exercise earlier in my career to help me and others navigate their career journey. This approach provides structure to the process so you will find your right fit and perhaps build courage along the way.

You can find more detailed instructions on how to complete your own Goldilocks framework in the working guide at the end of this book.

> A word of caution—this exercise is not always easy. Some people I have coached found that this exercise took them a couple of months to complete. They created several versions. They had to dig in and discern what put them on their path to where they are today and what is the right path for them going forward. They had to decide what they wanted for themselves versus what others expected of them. The secret is that the Goldilocks approach can help you at any stage of your career or during any changes in life.

After completing this exercise, one person I mentored quit their vice president of marketing role and decided to go to law school at age 38. That clarity of purpose, and of their path, gave them so much joy—it was wonderful to be a small part of their journey. That pivot in their career gave

Values	Motivators (life and work)	Superpowers	Emerging skills: Learning/new experiences	Desired future skills, goals, and experiences	Current job/life scenario
The core principles that truly matter in life and guide your behavior and decision-making	*The driving forces behind your actions, answering the why and energizing you to get up each day*	*These strengths are the sunshine in your positive shadow. They're what you love to do and what others rely on you for.*	*These are skills you've been building in the last year or so.*	*These are skills and experiences you're curious about and wish to explore.*	*Outline what you have now and indicate elements of joy versus those that might drain your energy.*
Growth	Financially independent—no debt (able to pay for kids' college)	Optimistic/ inspiring—sets vision for team	Supporting a new function—marketing	Live in a different country	Senior financial analyst—not making enough $ to cover college

Values	Motivators (life and work)	Superpowers	Emerging skills: Learning/new experiences	Desired future skills, goals, and experiences	Current job/life scenario
Freedom	Flexible schedule to support family needs	Excellent analytical skills	Learn and leverage artificial intelligence capability for analytics/insights	Learn a new language—most of our employees speak Spanish	Need to be in the office 5 days a week—no flex
Help/develop others	Leader at work	Organized/strong program management skills—gets stuff done!	Public speaking	Become a manager of a team	Take a management course

them joy, it aligned with their personal purpose/motivators, it gave them the quality of life they desired, and it gave them significant confidence. They were pursuing their right fit. Another leader just informed me that she uses the Goldilocks approach with her entire direct team. They use it to discuss career aspirations and development plans and build a tighter community that supports each other in their goals.

Maryanne (aka MAV) Viegelmann, earlier in her career and then a new mom, also embraced her inner Goldilocks. She was working at LinkedIn at the time and leveraged the Goldilocks approach when deciding if she should leave the company and what to do next. This exercise compassed both her career aspirations and how she could adjust to the changing demands in her personal life.

In her words, she stated that her coworkers and manager "were trying to help lead me. They all had great intentions to be helpful. However, I decided to lead myself. Each time I have decided for myself and went through my own reflection of my strengths and weaknesses while listening to my gut for the right next 'fit' I became more confident and happier." The magic, she said, was the opportunity to reflect and sometimes face internal truths head on. This process made the decision-making easier and helped her pivot with more confidence.

Career Development Lessons from Goldilocks

"If you don't know where you want to go, then it doesn't matter which path you take."
—The Cheshire Cat in *Alice in Wonderland*
by Lewis Carroll

Getting back to "Goldilocks and the Three Bears" for a moment, I summarized several micro lessons (aka the moral of the story) for your review, and hopefully for your benefit, in this section:

- *Self-awareness and exploration:* Goldilocks' journey represents the exploration phase of career development. Explore! There is no right or wrong or even a single path. Every path holds incredible learning opportunities. Goldilocks tries different things (porridge, chairs, even their beds) to discover what feels "just right" for her. You should explore, too.

  Along your journey, engage in self-reflection to uncover your strengths, interests, and values. You can probably feel your energy rise or fall depending on the work or the experience you are facing. These signals are important. Don't ignore them. Write them down. They indicate "fit."

  Be aware that there isn't a typical career path for so many roles, nor is there a single path in life. Let go of a preconceived path—be curious, be humble, and learn. Learn what works for you and what doesn't.

Time in Role

My Uncle Roland shared his wisdom when I began my career. He said,

Patty, year one of any role is just "flirting" with the role. You are learning the language and tools and getting a sense of the environment and beginning to solve problems, observing how others create solutions.

(continued)

(continued)

Year two, you are reflecting, fixing your own mistakes, and going deeper into that skill—having a broader impact and increasing your confidence.

Year three is when you are considered an "expert" in that craft. You can begin to see around corners. You actively seek to improve elements of the role to increase satisfaction or execution.

The risk: he cautioned me that if I stayed in a role more than three years, it would be more challenging to be seen as a fit for other career paths, regardless of the transferable skills. That others around you would only see you in that one dimension—not seeing that you are capable of doing other things in your future.

If you apply this to the fable, year one you try Papa Bear's chair but it feels hard and really big! You need to stretch! Year two, you are settling into Momma Bear's chair for a bit; it is comfortable but still a bit too large. In year three, you are sitting in Baby Bear's chair, feeling fully relaxed, confident. It is a "just right" fit. You fill the chair, are seen as the subject matter expert, and are confident and ready for a new adventure or more responsibility.

Food for thought: decide along your journey whether you want to flirt with a skill, be confident, or become the expert in whatever skill or experience you are pursuing at that time. You get to decide—it's your journey.

- *Recognizing individual preferences and needs:* Each bear had different preferences for their porridge and chairs, reflecting the unique needs and desires of individuals. Goldilocks also realized that not "any chair would do." One size does not fit all.

Similarly, you should recognize that your career aspirations and priorities in life may differ from your peers. In fact, no two people live their lives exactly alike. We are unique. Therefore, it is important to chart a course that aligns with your personal goals and values, rather than blindly following societal expectations, manager expectations, or others' expectations.

- *Ethical conduct and respect:* Because I don't condone breaking and entering in any scenario, I wanted to address this one element or moral point of the story. Goldilocks's actions disregard the bears' property and privacy. This element of the story reminds me of the importance of ethical conduct in career development. Respecting others, adhering to professional standards, and maintaining integrity are essential to building trust and reputation, leading to long-term career success. Her apology represents learning and accountability for one's actions.

  Are you perhaps a leader in your organization? Goldilocks had a few correlating leadership lessons. If you are a leader, consider the morals of the story from a leadership perspective.

Leading Others: Lessons from Goldilocks

The importance of finding the right fit for your team members is also key to building high performing teams:

- *Situational leadership:* Just as Goldilocks sought the porridge, chair, and bed that were "just right" for her, effective leaders understand the importance of tailoring their approach to fit individual needs and preferences for the employees on their teams.

- *Embracing differences:* Creating a workplace environment that creates a sense of belonging, and supports diversity and inclusion, where every individual feels valued and are able to thrive, is key. This means adapting your style to adjust for how they learn and how best to motivate them. Learn the nuance of unlocking their unique potential.

- *Go beyond the role:* Get to know the human side of your employees. This includes recognizing the unique strengths and weaknesses of team members, understanding their motivations, and adapting communication and task assignments accordingly.

Reflection: Building Your Goldilocks Framework

Did Goldilocks speak to you? (Some days I can't stop her from talking in my head!) What were the key elements that resonated the most? If you have a career plan, have you considered your motivators and your values? As you reflect on your superpowers, do they reflect what others say about you? What do they rely on you for? Have you explored what you want to learn or experience next?

In Summary: Finding Your Just Right Fit

Ultimately, Goldilocks finds the perfect porridge and chair, representing the ideal career match or step on her personal journey. I encourage you to strive to find a career and/or life path that feels "just right," aligning with your passions, skills, and values. This involves trying different roles, seeking feedback, and adjusting your career trajectory or life habits as needed.

> Remember, the "just right" path is not a static destination, but rather a dynamic journey of self-discovery, learning, and growth. Think about where you are on your life's journey and career path and where your possible next adventures lie. Are you ready to explore, reflect, and map your path?

By recognizing and applying these lessons, not only will you have a higher knowledge of self but you'll also be able to navigate the complexities of career development and life with greater clarity, purpose, joy, and ultimately achieve your desired aspirations. To assist you on this journey, check out the workbook guide at the end of this book.

My last piece of advice on your career or life plan is to set a plan. Determine *your* destination. That focus will unlock more magic than you can imagine. Having a plan goes hand-in-hand with setting your goals, which is covered next in Chapter 4. There you will get to meet the three little pigs. They will guide you on the power of setting goals.

The Three Little Pigs

Tapping into the Power of Goals

*O*nce upon a time, three little pigs were ready to leave their mother to build their own homes. They were all super excited for the adventure and, more important, their independence. Although they were brothers, each one approached this next milestone a little bit differently.

The youngest son, Sam, was a bit lazy and impatient. He threw together a flimsy straw house. He wanted to start partying with his friends or relax in the sun! The middle-born, Paul, was slightly more diligent. He constructed a house of sticks. Paul liked to sunbathe in the yard but also wanted a house that he would be proud to take his friends to. The oldest, Fred, was conscientious and hardwork-ing. Fred was thinking about the future. He knew that the woods could be dangerous, and he wanted to ensure the safety of his family. As a result, he decided to build a sturdy brick house. This took a lot longer to build, and it cost more than what Fred had in his savings. Fred also had to work part-time jobs to help pay for the building materials, which slowed down the construction of his home. Although he wanted to travel, have friends over, and play Xbox, he remained focused on the future. With his plan in place, Fred watched his two brothers relax and sunbathe while he continued to build his home and ultimately built the house he envisioned.

One day, a cunning and hungry wolf appeared, demanding entry into each pig's house—starting with the two youngest brothers. The wolf was very hungry. Although the pigs were scared, they refused the wolf's request. After each refusal, the wolf filled his lungs, huffed and puffed, easily blowing down the straw and stick houses. Thankfully, Paul and Sam were fast, and they hurriedly sought refuge *in their brother's brick house. Then the wolf approached the last home—Fred's brick home. The wolf attempted to huff and puff and when that failed, he tried to enter through the chimney.*

No matter what the wolf did, the house stood tall. When the wolf tried to sneak into the house, Fred once more outsmarted the wolf. He had a plan. He began boiling a pot of water in the fireplace, sending the wolf fleeing with singed fur.

The three pigs, now united and safe in the brick house, celebrated their victory over the wolf. Once the danger was behind them, Sam and Paul went to work raising money to build their own houses of brick. They learned from their older brother Fred, and sought his guidance on how to build the best home for their futures—safe from the big bad wolf.

Soon all three brothers had houses of brick and they lived happily ever after, safe in the big woods.

It's All About Setting Goals

This story resonates with me for various reasons. When I asked people in my network what the moral of this story was, a few reflected on the compassion the older brother had in taking care of his family. Others called out the strategic thinking and planning required to know what was needed to prepare for that potentially dangerous future. Still others mentioned Fred's dedication to his goal—putting off immediate satisfaction to plan and work toward a safer future. That took tenacity.

I love all of those elements. However, for me, it was the power of setting goals and being dedicated to them that resonated the most. Let's face it: it is hard to set long-term goals and stay focused on them. In this story, the older brother Fred knew what he needed to do to be safe and worked toward that goal. The other brothers also had goals—albeit more about relaxation and perhaps hanging out with their friends. (Although one could argue that the brothers' goals were perhaps not the wisest, all three pigs achieved their goals. What they envisioned they created.)

Fundamentally, *the power of setting goals is a significant catalyst that drives your decisions and behaviors.* If you have clarity on what you want to achieve, you can plan the necessary steps, evaluate your progress, and course correct when needed. You also have full ownership and accountability. You set the stage and you determine what success looks like.

Start with the End in Mind: Reverse Engineering

Fred, the brother who knew to build the house of bricks, had an end goal in mind. Do you know where you want to end? The finish line. Have you ever attempted to write your own obituary? Or visualize your ultimate career role? I did this in my visualization exercise with my coach. If you know the end goal and the time frame in which you want to achieve that goal, you can reverse engineer your path backwards to today and plan your journey moving forward.

Think of this process in this fashion: imagine you have a finished product, like a delicious cake. Reverse engineering a goal is like figuring out the recipe to bake that cake. Here's how it works:

1. *Start with the finished product:* This is your goal, the delicious cake you want to achieve.

2. *Break it down into steps:* Think about all the things that go into making the cake—mixing the batter, baking the cake, and frosting the cake. These are the smaller, more manageable steps you need to take. (Think micro goals!)

3. *Identify the ingredients:* What do you need for each step? Flour, sugar, eggs for the batter, oven time for baking, and so on. These are the resources and skills you need to complete each step.

4. *Work backwards:* Now you know the steps and ingredients, figure out how to do each step in the right order.

By reverse engineering your goal, you take a big, daunting goal and break it down into smaller, achievable tasks. This makes it easier to understand what you need to do and how to get there, one step at a time. It's like having a road map to reach your delicious cake (the goal)!

Our Brains Encourage Us to Create Goals

I love our brains! We are all unique. Being neurodiverse made me naturally curious about how my brain operates. Along that journey of self-discovery, I learned that there are so many neurodiverse people in the world, and it is magical to see how our unique relationship with our brain manifests in different behaviors and feelings.

Considering Neurodiversity

Let's step back a minute and reflect on what I mean when I say neurodiverse. *Neurodiversity* refers to the idea that human brains function in a wide variety of ways, and these variations are not inherently pathological. It encompasses conditions like ADHD (attention deficit hyperactivity disorder), ASD (autism spectrum disorder), dyslexia, and dyspraxia. Let's look at how neurodiversity can affect how our brains think and react to the world.

Information Processing

- Some neurodiverse brains might be *hyper*sensitive or *hypo*sensitive to sensory input like sound, light, touch, taste, or smell. This can lead to overload or under-stimulation, affecting focus and interaction with the environment.

- Attention and focus can also be affected. Conditions like ADHD might make it difficult to filter out distractions, and ASD can lead to hyperfocus on specific interests.

Social Interaction and Communication

- ASD can make it challenging to understand social cues, unwritten rules, and nonverbal communication. This can lead to social awkwardness or difficulty forming relationships.

- Processing language can also be different. People with dyslexia might struggle with reading fluency, and those with autism might have trouble with the pragmatics of language, like using humor or sarcasm.

(continued)

The Three Little Pigs

(continued)

Cognitive Strengths

- Neurodiversity also comes with unique strengths. People with ADHD might have exceptional creativity and problem-solving skills.

- Those on the autism spectrum might excel at detail-oriented tasks, have strong memories, or demonstrate in-depth knowledge in specific areas.

Emotional Processing

- Emotional regulation can be a challenge for some neurodiverse individuals. Difficulty interpreting social cues or managing sensory overload can lead to anxiety or meltdowns.

It's important to remember that neurodiversity is a spectrum. Everyone experiences these variations in brain function to a different degree. Understanding how your brain works can help you find strategies to manage challenges and leverage your strengths. Learning about my dyslexia helped me determine different strategies to read, process information, and navigate math.

Even taking neurodiversity into account, there are some common elements in how all of our brains react. For example, in Chapter 1 I shared how you react to hearing a story. In this chapter, I want to explore how your brain reacts to setting goals. Research revealed some surprising truths and helpful strategies for goal setting. The following sections break down the key principles.

Setting Goals Provides Motivation and Reward

The neurotransmitter dopamine plays a crucial role in motivation and reward. Setting and achieving goals triggers dopamine release, creating a satisfying loop that encourages further goal setting.

Prompt: Do you create checklists of work that you need to do each day? I do. Those daily activities are micro goals. The best part about that list is when I get to check off the items I have accomplished. Why? Because of that amazing dopamine rush. That rush fuels me to focus on the next goal. I love a checklist! Try it out.

The prefrontal cortex and the basal ganglia collaborate to plan, initiate, and monitor progress toward goals. These areas activate during goal setting, reflecting the brain's investment in pursuing the desired outcome. They are goal-oriented systems and serve as good motivators.

Prompt: That checklist I mentioned? When I break down my goals into tangible daily, weekly, or monthly tasks, I get to check them off on completion. These micro goals lead to the achievement of my bigger goal. Think about completing a course in school—check! Or getting certified in a particular skill—check! Working on your professional network to help find your next gig—check! These micro achievements give you confidence to achieve your macro goals. Try it out!

Getting into the Zone!

To achieve your goals, you need focus and attention. Our brains help provide such focus in several ways:

- *Neurotransmitters like norepinephrine and acetylcholine help focus our attention:* These neurotransmitters play a vital role in focusing attention and filtering out distractions. When setting goals, these systems are activated, enhancing our ability to concentrate on the necessary steps to achieve them.

- This definitely works for me! I get a surge of energy once I sit down and work on my goals. Specifically, when I get to focus on my Goldilocks framework, it feels like time just flies. I get into a zone. My hypothesis is that if you are creating a personal goal, such as determining your career path or creating your financial plans, you are more likely to get into that focused zone.

- *Visualizations and mental imagery help with motivation:* Imagining yourself successfully achieving a goal activates similar brain regions as actually achieving it, potentially boosting motivation and setting the stage for success.

My Visualization and Goals

In fall 2002, I was a senior director of HR. At that time, I was working with Denise, my coach, to focus on my leadership journey to become a chief human resources (HR) officer.

One weekend, Denise invited five women to a leadership development in Sausalito, California. We were working together to craft our personal vision and create our three-year career journey map. The visualization exercise was the most impactful part of that weekend.

Denise led us through a process where we closed our eyes. She asked us to visualize a point in the future when we had achieved our career goal.

As she guided us, she asked the following questions:

- What would our office look like?
- What would we see when we walked down the hallway?
- How would people interact with us?
- How would we feel?
- What would we be working on?

The questions got more detailed as time went on. In the process, I visualized the following:

I had an original painting of purple flowers in a cool vase (that I had yet to paint!) hung up on the wall of my office. It reminded me of van Gogh. On my desk were pictures of my husband and kids. I pictured them older, playing sports. When I walked around the building, people smiled at me. They invited me to eat lunch with them. I felt both needed and wanted. On my desk were files and a presentation that I was preparing to give to the board.

When I opened my eyes, I realized that time had flown by! In the 90-minute session, I got the clarity I needed for my future. I was inspired. I wanted my employees to see my creativity in the painting, to know about my family and create a trusted relationship so that I could learn about theirs. The employee smiles in the hallway made me feel welcomed and that I belonged. I sensed that my work mattered, and that they appreciated it. The files and presentation on my desk reminded me of the responsibility I had to the company. That the work mattered to our board and shareholders.

(continued)

(continued)

Fast forward one year later, to 2004. I achieved my career goal. I became a chief HR officer at Align Technology.

The first thing I did was paint that painting I had seen in my vision and place it on my office wall. (That painting now hangs in my house these many years later to remind me of the power of visualization!) Next were the pictures of my family on my desk. My vision was beginning to be realized. That moment was surreal for me. To visualize an event and see it come true was magical. As I continue to pursue my career, or chase big audacious goals, I now spend time upfront visualizing what success can look and feel like. It gives me the clarity and confidence to move forward.

Courtesy of Pat Wadors, artist.

What have you visualized?

Overcoming Challenges

Any big goal has challenges, and working toward big audacious goals can be stressful. I knew I had the right "mountain," aka goal, but my path up the mountain was not always clear. Several boulders were placed along my path! I made mistakes. It was sometimes scary, stressful, and humbling. It was also an amazing education!

What can you expect and do when facing a challenge along your path?

- *Amygdala and stress response:* When faced with obstacles or setbacks, the amygdala triggers the stress response, hindering performance. However, mindfulness and stress management techniques help regulate the amygdala and maintain focus on the goal, despite challenges embracing a growth mindset! That mindset will reduce the stress response.

- *Resilience and neuroplasticity:* The brain has incredible plasticity, meaning it can adapt and change in response to experiences. Setting and achieving goals, even with setbacks, strengthens neural connections and builds resilience, making you better equipped to handle future challenges. Truthfully, every mistake and challenge has made me stronger. It might not have been easy in the moment, but those moments built strength and wisdom that I am able leverage to achieve my goals.

Effective Goal-Setting Strategies

I am sure Fred, the eldest brother, followed these steps and tips to achieve his goal of keeping his family safe in a brick house. As you craft your goals, keep these tips in mind:

- *Set SMART goals:* Setting specific, measurable, achievable, relevant, and time-bound goals helps focus efforts and track progress.

- *Break goals down into smaller micro steps:* Think about your daily checklist. Dividing tasks into manageable tasks makes them less overwhelming.

- *Celebrate milestones:* Stay motivated! Taking time to acknowledge and appreciate your progress releases dopamine and reinforces positive, goal-oriented behavior.

- *Visualize success and your path:* Use mental imagery to see yourself achieving your goal, which can activate brain regions associated with actual success and boost motivation.

- *Focus on the process/learning along the way:* Prioritize enjoying the journey toward your goal rather than solely fixating on the end macro goal. This reduces stress and promotes a more sustainable approach.

By understanding the neuroscience behind goal setting, you can craft strategies that tap into your brain's reward systems, enhance focus, and build resilience for optimal goal achievement.

The Pursuit of Goals Has Its Own Reward

The journey is just as important as the destination, so enjoy the process, celebrate your progress, and let neuroscience guide you to success! In pursuing your goals, you will learn a bit more about yourself—from your mistakes as well as from your achievements. Without the journey and the lessons learned, it is unlikely that you can achieve your desired goals.

In practical terms, the journey prepares you for achieving your goals with quality.

My Goals

Unlike Fred in "The Three Little Pigs," I did not have a long-term goal as I was growing up. I was focused on the here and now. With my learning challenges, I just needed to pass my classes so I would not get into trouble. Passing the class with a C was enough. I did not believe at that time that I could get higher grades. False constraints—limiting beliefs of self in my head—kept me from dreaming bigger dreams.

In fact, one day in sixth grade—facing another awful spelling test—I wrote the 10 spelling words on the palm of my right hand (I'm a lefty!) before school started so I would be sure to pass my class. I had to get a C or above to pass. In a sad twist of fate, when I turned in my paper, my teacher immediately graded it and I got a D. How could that be? I was so upset I showed my teacher that I had cheated and still FAILED THE TEST! Needless to say, she changed my grade to an F and I got into deeper

(continued)

(continued)

trouble at home. No one questioned how I could have failed a test that I cheated on—even my teacher.

Although I continued to struggle, the moral of that experience was that cheating was not a shortcut to my success (*is it ever?*). Hard work, leveraging my strengths, and seeking support from others was my path forward. It was a lesson I was grateful to learn early on in life.

Big Goals Come with Challenges and Self-Doubt

I had self-doubt many times along my journey. In the early 1980s, the position of chief HR, or rather head of personnel, was held mainly by men. My uncle pointed that fact out to me and tried to steer me to be a recruiter or a benefits analyst. Although those roles would be part of my journey, they were not my end destination. I understood that he was attempting to manage my expectations, but his words fired me up. I wanted to experience every major facet of my profession. The craft of HR excited me. I wanted to break the stereotype. I also wanted to prove that being dyslexic wasn't going to stop me.

Get an Accountability Partner!

To counter the self-doubt, I encourage you to get an accountability partner. Goals are important to have, but sharing your goal with others can increase your personal accountability toward that goal. When you share your goals, it can make them more real.

In my case, with support and leveraging the tenacity I learned while navigating my learning differences in school, I kept on track with my plans. But the biggest surprise came from my accountability network: my dad; my best friend, Richea; my coach, Denise; and my Uncle Roland. They checked in on me periodically and that meant the world to me. They believed in me. I am sure the accountability partner whom you choose will also believe in you. Maybe they will see more in you than you see in yourself!

With a Little Help from Your Friends and Mentors

Audacious goals take time, and we all need help along the way. In "The Three Little Pigs" fable, think how the oldest brother Fred helped his two brothers build their safer homes. He helped them set and achieve their goals. Don't be afraid to ask for help and mentoring. With the support of my mentors, managers, coaches, family, and friends, I navigated my career and life decisions to achieve my goals. The friends I made, the coworkers who showed me the ropes, the confidence I built, the mistakes I made (and those who forgave me), and the resulting doses of humility along the way was a journey. That journey was just as rewarding as the title I finally achieved when I was 39 years old. It was and continues to be the journey that shapes who I am today. Both the good and the more challenging events.

Setting my audacious goal and being dedicated to the pursuit of that goal was the catalyst to my success. But believing in myself and learning from others gave me the resilience in that pursuit.

The Power of Friendship

When I was going through the loss of my mom, I was blessed to have the unconditional support and love from my best friend, Richea. I met her during my freshman year in high school in Shreveport, Louisiana. We have been best friends ever since, and she has become an accountability partner as well. She was with me when my mom passed, and more recently when my dad passed. Richea supports me when I struggle, forgives me when I make mistakes, pushes me to be better, keeps me humble, and makes me laugh until I cry.

When I share my goals with her, she does not laugh or challenge the possibility of that goal. She quietly, completely believes in me. Richea has also joined me along my journey. She has visited me at work numerous times, joined me on a business trip in Costa Rica, and boosted my confidence when I felt low. Having her by my side has made me more resilient. She also reminds me that being authentically me was enough to achieve my goals.

Having a friend like that in life is such a gift. Richea— thank you for believing in me and my goals! You just need that one special person to believe in you, and the world of possibilities becomes more real. Richea is that special person for me!

Avoid comparing your goals with your peers. You are unique—in skills, passion, and grit.

"What works for one, may not work for another."
—Akiroq Brost

In Summary: Setting Flexible Goals

Ultimately as you know, all three pigs achieved their goals. Two of the brothers had to modify their goals based on lessons and coaching from their brother. That is normal! Goals should not be stagnant. As with the Goldilocks exercise, I encourage you to revisit your goals and the paths you are taking to achieve those goals. The mountain (i.e. the audacious goal) might stay the same, but with wisdom, you might discover a different path or shorter-term goals that work just right for you.

Now you are ready to visualize your future and chart your course. Following are tips to help you chart your path and set your goals.

- *Strategic planning/defining success in the long term:*
  - *Think forward in years—then reverse engineer the path:* What is your end destiny? If your vision/plan is set in days, week, months, or even quarters, you might miss the bigger opportunities that await you or the potential challenges in later years. To craft your path, I suggest you *reverse engineer your legacy story—start with the end goal in mind and chart your path in reverse year by year.* Then begin to write down your steps toward those shorter goals that align to your end destination or big audacious goal.
  - *Share your plan:* Do the hard work and stay focused on the goal and the why behind that goal. You will be surprised at your energy, creativity, and willingness to do the hard work that comes from setting a personal goal.
  - *Align your goals to your values and your passion.* By doing this, you will create goals that motivate you and give you the courage to stay focused and learn from your mistakes: Fred lived his values—family first—by taking care of his family. That motivation is an essential ingredient to resilience and a growth mindset.
- *Role modeling, teaching, and compassion:*
  - In "The Three Little Pigs," Fred, the brother who built the house of bricks, welcomed his brothers into his home when they had nowhere else to turn. Fred did not chastise his brothers, instead he was there with an open door, a safe haven. As a leader,

Fred remained agile/focused until everyone was safe. Afterwards, he mentored his brothers, helping them build sturdier houses. As a result, they all got to live happily ever after.

For me, I love being a teaching leader. I take time to share the context for my decisions, and I share my mistakes (and they have been many!) and the learnings with my team, my children, and mentees. When mistakes happen, I reiterate that it is not the mistake that should be the focal point, it should be what you got to learn and how you pick yourself up from those mistakes.

> This is an important point. Learn from your mistakes. Don't shy away from challenges. Frame your mindset to "guess what I learned today?" It will energize you. I love the learning that comes from those experiences.

My hope is that you are now inspired to craft your big audacious goal(s), have the grit and courage to face your challenges, and perhaps achieve your success with more joy—*living happily ever after.*

In the next chapter, you learn how to create your personal scorecard, which pulls together the insights you gained from your Goldilocks exercise and combines it with your stated goals. I'm excited for you to learn about the gifts a personal scorecard will bring to your life.

Chapter 5

The Tortoise and the Hare

Embracing Your Personal Scorecard

*O*nce upon a time, a tortoise and a hare met up in the woods. They looked at each other with curiosity. They were very different from each other. The tortoise was slow and steady, and the hare was fast and impulsive. One was tall, the other short. The hare loved to compete and show off; he had a lot of confidence. He would brag to his forest friends about his speed—his superpower. He would also say disparaging comments about the slow tortoise. The tortoise was quieter—you could say introverted. She liked a slower lifestyle, but she was also confident. She loved a good competition, all in good fun. She was not one to brag nor was she someone who put others down. She was steady.

One day, after several nudges and teasing by the hare, the tortoise agreed to have a race. Their forest friends were surprised about this turn of events! The hare, being confident that he would win, took off running as fast as he could, looking back only once, so sure he would win. Within seconds, the spectators could no longer see the hare. The tortoise, however, took her time and walked slowly but steadily. She thanked her friends for watching the race. She reminded them that she loved to compete and that she saw this race as an adventure.

After a while, the hare got tired from running so fast and decided to take a nap. He used up a lot of energy showing off in the beginning of the race. The hare thought that the tortoise was very far behind him, so he didn't worry about losing. He assumed he could wake up after a quick power nap and go on to win the race easily. Meanwhile, the tortoise kept walking and eventually passed the hare while he was asleep. The tortoise saw the hare sleeping, but she didn't slow down or make fun of the hare. She just kept walking.

The hare—sleeping longer than he envisioned— eventually woke up and was surprised to see turtle tracks in

71

the dirt next to him. He realized that the tortoise had passed him by! In fact, he couldn't even see the tortoise from where he was standing. In a panic, he tried to catch up, but the tortoise was too far ahead.

In the end, as you can probably guess, the tortoise won the race. Friends from the forest surrounded the tortoise congratulated her on her success and asked what her secret was. How did she outrun the hare? The hare, still in disbelief, also wanted to hear the tortoise's secret. The hare realized that speed may be a superpower, but it isn't sufficient without other attributes like focus, humility, and grit.

Why a Personal Scorecard?

I love sharing this story, as it brings back early childhood memories. And yes, like my Nanny use to do, I took the liberty of sharing my own version of this famous fable. The story arc and the moral lesson, however, remain the same as the original telling. The biggest lesson I took away was that the tortoise clearly lived her life her way. She had her own personal scorecard. In knowing herself and her own scorecard, the tortoise did not let others push her to being something she was not. She lived according to her values. She won.

But what is a personal scorecard?

A *personal scorecard* is the balance between the *what* (your goals and metrics) and the *how* (expected behaviors and values you pursue in life).

A scorecard pulls together the insights you gained from your Goldilocks exercise and combines it with your stated goals. In this example, the tortoise had a goal to win the race. She won by being true to herself. She believed in being authentic, running the race at her pace, and staying focused.

This should not be a scorecard of how others measure you, but how you measure yourself. It becomes a compass, guiding you in decisions and behaviors.

With the tortoise as our role model, the purpose of this chapter is to help you explore your personal scorecard at work, home, and in your community. The point is not to wait until your story is finished to judge how well you lived it. The goal is to gain clarity on the what (the quest) and the how (the journey of living your best life).

The First Stage: Know Yourself and What Makes You Proud of Being You

When I was young, I never truly felt like I belonged. I struggled with school, but instead of exploring my challenges, my parents, teachers, and perhaps my friends and siblings thought I was just being lazy or just not smart enough. They stopped encouraging me to be more. At times, I let their labels become the story I told myself.

Eventually, I discovered that I hated the labels others gave me. Somewhere—deep down—I felt that I had more than they knew. I refused to accept their labels, their scorecard of me. I was motivated to develop my own sense of success. For me, that clarity would give me a sense of confidence, purpose, and a bit of control.

Ignite Your Inner Fire: The Key to Unlocking Your Potential

Knowing your goals is a great first step, but it's only part of the journey to becoming your best self. I've discovered that true success hinges on two additional superpowers: *self-awareness* and *self-accountability*.

Imagine these three elements working together:

- *Intrinsic drive:* This is the motivation that fuels you from within, not external pressures. It's about doing things because you find them fulfilling, fun, and meaningful.

- *Inner fire:* This is your passion, your why. It's the spark that ignites your drive and keeps you enthusiastic even when things get tough.

- *Self-directedness:* This is your ability to take charge, set your own goals, and adjust your course when needed. You're the captain of your ship, making sure your actions align with your values and aspirations.

Connecting these three elements in your scorecard is a game-changer. Not many people take the time to truly understand these elements within themselves. When they do take the time—wow. I see it all the time when interviewing potential employees. It is a powerful, attractive trait that sets top talent apart. They have the clarity of motivation and purpose. As a result, their ability to inspire others and build relationships is amazing.

Inner Fire in Action: My Son Eddie's Story

My son Eddie is a perfect example. His passion for science has been his why since childhood. He lives authentically, driven by his own internal compass. When he faced a recent challenge—a layoff—his inner fire became his guiding light.

He took this opportunity to be brutally honest with himself. What did he truly value? What kind of role would ignite his passion? By getting clear on his why and what roles aligned with his values, he embarked on a successful job search. Although the search took a bit longer, his inner fire fueled his confidence and engagement during interviews, resulting in a "just right" fit.

The Power of Self-Awareness and Self-Accountability

Eddie's story showcases for me the power of self-awareness and self-accountability. By understanding his strengths and passions and staying true to his values, he navigated a difficult situation with purpose. When he felt defeated and considered other paths, he just revisited his own scorecard and stayed resolute.

Unleash Your Inner Fire

Remember, you have this inner fire within you, too. Take some time to reflect and understand your why. What ignites your passion? What fuels your motivation? Once you tap into that fire, you'll be unstoppable! These elements should be captured in your Goldilocks framework.

Discovering Me Took Time

I am creative, so I pursued art. I loved to read, so I read most days. I am competitive, so I played sports. I hate math, but I couldn't avoid the periodic required math classes in school. I love to dance, but sometimes my rhythm is off 😕. I want to belong. I want to matter.

In search of that, I hung out with different groups of friends throughout my life, striving to find my tribe. Looking for people who let me be me and who liked me as me and made me stronger. I also learned along my journey of discovery that I wasn't lazy when it came to learning. With my disability, I discovered that I had a strong work ethic. In school, I would put in extra work to get Cs or above. I was self-motivated and worked hard to prove to myself that I could succeed. Not to please anyone else. Those early elements were the start of my own scorecard and remain with me today.

Essentially, I was striving to become the best version of me that I could be. Someone I was proud to be. I just wasn't sure at all times what or how to achieve those end goals, but I felt that I was on the right path. I felt that clarity mattered. With that clarity of goals and who I believed I was, I could shut out the other voices pushing me or judging me against a scorecard that was not mine. I would surround myself with friends and family who gave me honest feedback, making me better. People who gave me the confidence to grow and quiet the gremlins of self-doubt.

My Scorecard

My personal scorecard includes my career goals, family goals, financial goals, and community goals. These goals have shifted in prioritization, and the goal posts have shifted over time as well. Sometimes one of those categories overshadowed the others when there was a need. For example, I purposefully took roles that didn't require travel even if it meant a promotion so that I could be close to my children when they were young. I slowed down my career goal. Another example was saving money, not going on big vacations, and eating at home, all so we could save money to buy a home. Looking at my scorecard and reflecting on my goals made decisions and priorities easier to make and set. I continue to review and redefine my scorecard as I age. It has been an amazing practice to help keep me focused on the right things at the right time.

Consider my scorecard to use as an example for creating your own:

Physical Health—Prioritize Better!
- Annual physical dr. appt! (don't reschedule!)
- Invisalign—wear retainers!
- Eat more plant-based foods weekly.
- Ride bikes with Dave every weekend! Explore SB.

Creative Outlets
- Paint 3–5 paintings this year.
- Teach a Braille Institute art class
- Do crafts/draw/color with my daughter as often as we can!
- Finish my book by mid-April. Yikes! (final edits by June)

Financial
- Get my LLC up and running.
- Determine retirement timeline/investment strategies—by Sept.
- Teach my kids the benefit to review taxes/plan to be homeowners, save $ for kids college, etc.

The Tortoise and the Hare

Family First—Always	Work	Community/Friends
• See grand-kids every 6–10 weeks! They grow fast.	• Navigate travel schedule—be with family on key dates (b'days/anniversaries/holidays)	• Intentionally create memory moments with friends every month! (so far so good this year!)
• Be in person to celebrate b'days.	• Onboard new leaders—build new team, ☺	• Visit Richea 1–2 x a year.
• Help w/ Eddie's wedding.	• Increase employee engagement on my team—5 pts.	• Donate/volunteer in the community. Braille Institute— winter semester— 7 days. (done)
• See siblings—celebrate our b'days/visit Dorothy (stepmom)—call/check in 1–2 a month.	• Advise/mentor others.	• Make friends! Stay connected more frequently—let them know that they matter to me.
• Explore volunteer work—Katie/build skills	• Visit Ireland/UK/India, and ANZ this year.	
• Dave and I explore SB/date—quality time.		

Creating a Scorecard as a Couple

As an adult, I evolved my scorecard elements. The elements changed in so many ways, personally and professionally. I got married, had three kids, a dog, and a career. Priorities shifted as our family expanded and got more complex. I made mistakes and learned from them. My scorecard became clearer and was even more powerful when it was shared as a couple and then as a family.

Our scorecard became the touchstone for how we make decisions as a family.

But let me take a quick step back. Like every couple, Dave and I had to adjust and pivot as we evolved as partners and as parents. Our third child, Katie, was born with special needs. She is neurodiverse and struggles to process and navigate complex situations. Estimating time and math are huge challenges for her. She also was developmentally delayed and struggled with speech for several years. Needless to say, her path, and ours as parents, is not an easy one to travel. Fortunately, Dave and I came together to build the initial foundation of our scorecard as a couple—to navigate Katie's needs as well as that of her two brothers. Our scorecard and our values led us on a healthier path together as a family.

Like I said, it's never an easy path with a child with special needs. It doesn't come with a playbook or a how-to guide. Most couples with children who have significant special needs end up in divorce—approximately 80%.[1] That statistic was a key intrinsic motivator for both of us to ensure we worked together and aligned on our values. Ultimately, it was our aligned values and goals in how we wanted to be as a family that kept us strong as a family. Katie has the best spirit. Her close relationship with her brothers brings all of us joy. She has made our family more compassionate, patient, humble (she always tells the truth!), and resilient. We know that we will always be there for each other. Family first is not only on our family scorecard but it was also the first tattoo that my eldest son got at age 18.

Our second major scorecard moment together was when my husband's dad was diagnosed with liver cancer.

He lived on his own, about an hour away from us. We didn't see him often due to the distance. We were also busy with our three kids and work. But Dave's dad got progressively worse. We felt that he could no longer live by himself. He needed help and care. He wanted more support.

We were struggling to find the right answer. What should we do? How can we take care of our family, our careers, and provide care for his dad? What was the right balance for us? Who can we depend on to help?

We discussed possible solutions with my husband's family. We believed that he could no longer live on his own and navigate his health care properly. My husband's family didn't see the situation as we did. They felt things could stay the same. As a result of their reluctance to partner with us on this issue, Dave didn't push to move his dad at that time. However, he struggled with that decision. He was frustrated. We were both worried. We were basically allowing others' actions, their decisions, to become ours. But was that the right approach? We found that we were struggling with our own values and what we needed to or should do.

Whose values should we follow? Ours or theirs?

One night, after several conversations on this topic, I asked Dave what his personal scorecard was and how our scorecard as a couple would influence our decision. What values does he want to live by? What actions in this situation would make him proud of himself at the end of his life's journey? What decision as a couple, parents to young kids, would model the behavior and values we wish for them to emulate? I stated that we shouldn't make decisions based on others' behaviors, values, or beliefs. Because if we don't live or strive to live our best version, we won't be happy and likely might end up with regrets and perhaps be poor role models for our children.

The lightning bolt hit! The decision suddenly became clear to both of us, thanks to our scorecard. We asked Dave's dad to live near us—a mile away. He agreed. We found a place for him to live, handled his move, stepped up the care, and kept a close eye out for any struggles. We did have challenges, but we also had wonderful family moments. Lunch at his favorite spot, Father's Day with our kids, and stories shared about his life. We helped him with his health journey. And we were there when he passed away peacefully in that new home in 2016 as he requested. We have no regrets because we lived by our scorecard.

Now, whenever Dave or I think have a tough decision to make, we discuss our personal scorecard. We share the elements that matter to us as a couple and as individuals. It has made us stronger as a team. It has brought us closer as a couple, because we help each other live up to our best version of self. He knows me better than anyone and I know him. We keep each other honest. What a gift.

Reflection: Creating Your Scorecard

As you reflect, look inside yourself and craft your own legacy. Your scorecard is your compass for your quest. Ask yourself:

- What is the moral of my story? What do I want to be known for? By my family, friends, work?
- Which of my values are non-negotiable?
- How do I define success?

(continued)

(continued)

- At the end of the day, do I like the decisions I have made and how I have behaved? If not, what should I do differently next time?

Write down your personal and professional goals and create defined timelines. Determine a frequency to check in on your scorecard.

Write those elements down and then begin striving to walk that path. You will be perfectly imperfect. But you will have clarity. You will be focused and purpose-driven. You will also be more accountable to yourself and to others as you share your scorecard. The best part is that those closest to you will encourage you on your path. In return, you will inspire others to be their best, most authentic selves.

Your personal scorecard is a tool for your own growth and development. There is no right or wrong way to do it. Customize it to reflect your values, unique goals, and aspirations, and use it as a guide to live a fulfilling and meaningful life. I encourage you to share relevant parts of your scorecard with those who are closest to you—at home or at work. Consider whether one or more of these people could be your accountability partner on your journey.

Sharing Your Scorecard

If you're comfortable, share your scorecard with your family and your coworkers. In fact, I share many of my personal scorecard elements with my team, the employees I care for, and my manager. It is one way for me to let them know me—the human. Not just my title. These are moments of vulnerability as I share these elements, but sharing also builds trust. I don't share every element of my scorecard, but I share enough so that they know my values and my expectations for myself. This provides a peek into how I lead others.

The Moral of the Tortoise's Scorecard

The tortoise had her own scorecard. She knew who she was and her superpowers. She was confident and believed in herself. She would stay focused on the goal at hand. She did not judge others by their appearance. She was not flustered by how others saw her. And she loved a good competition. Ultimately, she followed her own scorecard with a clear focus on the following:

- *Know your personal scorecard:* The tortoise's unwavering self-belief and clarity on expectations, despite the hare's mockery and underestimation, underscores the role of perseverance and authenticity in leadership. Strong leaders (of self and others) maintain a resolute belief in their abilities and goals, a commitment to their values, and expectations of self even in the face of setbacks, pushback, or skepticism.

- *Stay focused:* The tortoise's unwavering focus on the objective, while the hare got sidetracked by distractions, emphasizes the importance of staying focused on the task at hand. Effective leaders maintain a clear vision and avoid getting derailed by external distractions or temptations.

- *Have humility and learn from your mistakes:* The hare's eventual acknowledgment of his overconfidence and underestimation of the tortoise serves as a reminder of the value of humility and learning from mistakes in leadership. Effective leaders recognize their limitations, embrace feedback, and continuously seek opportunities for improvement.

At the end of the fable we know that the tortoise won the race that really mattered. Not the race with the hare, but the race of personal success achieved her way.

A Compass for Life: Prioritizing What Matters Most

Year-end reflection is a powerful tool for me. It's a chance to assess how I "showed up"—the choices I made, the actions I took, and the paths not chosen. Looking back on 2023, a year filled with challenges, I can confidently say I lived by my personal scorecard—my guiding light.

Early in my new role as chief people officer at UKG, a leadership event in Orlando conflicted with a planned visit to see my 94-year-old dad. A rare moment of uncharacteristic worry from him sent a wave of concern. True to my scorecard, I prioritized family. I drove to see him, witnessing the progression of his dementia and poor health, and sharing my concerns with my stepmom, Dorothy.

The doctor's recommendation for hospice shortly after that visit was a gut punch. Emotions ran high, memories flooded back, and precious limited time with Dad became a looming reality. To find solace, I turned to art that day, a practice that nourishes my soul. The result is a vibrant flower painting hanging on my wall in my office that represents his spirit and our shared love of the ocean.

Change was inevitable. My scorecard provided clarity: family comes first. My new company and team, to my immense gratitude, were incredibly supportive as I rearranged my schedule to be there for my dad and Dorothy. Work took a backseat, some balls were dropped, but they bounced back. Sleep and exercise fell by the wayside. Delayed flights and missing my family were also all part of the experience, but the trade-offs were well worth it. I got to hold my dad's hand a dozen times, share precious memories, bake his favorite cookies, spend quality time with my siblings, and give support to Dorothy. The choices were sometimes difficult, but ultimately they were the right ones for me.

He passed peacefully on May 8, 2023, just shy of his 95th birthday, surrounded by love. I miss you, Pops!

This experience reinforces the importance of having a personal compass. It guides us to prioritize what truly matters, even when faced with tough decisions. We all face challenges, but by reflecting and setting intention, we can navigate life's journey with purpose and compassion.

In Summary: It's Your Scorecard

I encourage you to take the time to reflect on the questions raised in this chapter and build your personal compass. If you have a partner, spend time figuring out your shared scorecard. You will be surprised at how that clarity will guide your path forward.

Your scorecard will evolve. It should include *what* you want to achieve and *how* you want to achieve it. Gaining that level of clarity is eye-opening and will help you with your decisions in life. When spinning on an issue, pull out your scorecard!

> Your scorecard should pull in the values that you identified in your Goldilocks framework. But, like "The Three Little Pigs" lesson, it should also have your near-term goals, which feed into your longer-range plans for your life and career. Those goals are milestones based on time and/or by outcomes.

Here are a few highlights to consider:

- *A scorecard encourages personal growth:* A personal scorecard for life and leadership is a powerful tool for self-reflection, goal setting, and growth. It provides clarity to what success looks like and helps you track your progress in various areas of your life—personal and professional—and identify areas for improvement.

- *Start with your vision:* Visualize your legacy. How did you make others feel? What do you want to achieve in your life? What's your ideal future? The moral of your story? Defining your vision/your life's story will guide your goals and priorities. Write these thoughts down! There are no wrong answers.

- *Identify your core values:* (Hint: You will need these on your Goldilocks exercise, too!) What are the principles that are most important to you? Integrity, adaptability, creativity, and so on. Your values will inform your decisions and actions. Our values sharpen as we age. Think about the elements of a company culture where you will do your best work, where you will get a sense of belonging.

- *Create life domains:* Divide your scorecard into different domains that matter most to you. This could include areas like physical health, mental well-being, personal relationships, career, financial security, and community outreach. You choose.

  Then set goals for each domain. What do you want to achieve in each area of your life? Where applicable, make your goals SMART (specific, measurable, achievable, relevant, and time-bound). Some elements like values are hard to measure, but you know what behavior that's in alignment with those values looks like when modeling or observing others.

- *Consider the leadership dimension:* Define your leadership vision and identify the skills and behaviors you want to develop or model. Ask yourself how you want those you lead to describe you. These aspects will help drive your leadership shadow. You can learn more about this aspect in Chapter 6.

- *Hold yourself accountable:* Assess yourself on the qualities you are pursuing. Seek feedback often! Sometimes we are blind to how our behaviors affect others. Review your scorecard daily, weekly, or periodically throughout the year. How about when you review your new year's resolutions? Annual performance review? Or when you have a new baby? Get married? If you lead a team, share what's on your personal scorecard and urge them to create their own. It will bring you closer together as a group and there will be no limit to what you can accomplish. Regularly review your scorecard and adjust it as needed.

Now, LET'S ROLL!

As each year draws to a close, it's a powerful time to reflect. For me, this means revisiting my personal scorecard—a framework that keeps me grounded and helps my family understand my priorities. And guess what? Sharing it with others strengthens their support for my path.

Here is the magical key: taking a moment to reflect. Carve out some quiet, focused time—you won't regret it! Ask yourself these questions:

- What truly matters to me in this season of life?
- What areas need more attention?
- How can I create a balanced and fulfilling road map for the future?

I wonder what answers will come to mind. There is no such thing as a wrong answer. Pay attention to those elements that give you energy, too. These elements will find their way into your scorecard—if they truly matter. Remember, whether you're a goal-oriented hare or a steady tortoise, the path to self-discovery is an adventure filled with lessons.

With this scorecard framework in hand, I'm excited for you to read the next chapter. There you will meet the emperor. He will guide you on the importance of feedback—the ability to really listen and seek feedback is crucial if you want to know if you are truly living according to your scorecard. Hint: Sometimes what you hear may not be what you want to hear. Now, if you are ready—turn the page! Another adventure awaits.

Note

1. Ann Gold Buscho, "Divorce and Special Needs Children," *Psychology Today,* https://www.psychologytoday.com/us/blog/a-better-divorce/202302/divorce-and-special-needs-childrenpen_spark.

The Emperor's New Clothes

Understanding Your Leadership Shadow

Once upon a time, in the sunny kingdom of Vanity lived an emperor obsessed with clothes. He spent all his time and money on the most extravagant outfits, not realizing he was neglecting his kingdom and his people. One day, two cunning swindlers arrived, claiming to weave magical fabric invisible to those "unfit for their positions" or "stupid." Seeing an opportunity to outshine everyone, the emperor eagerly hired them.

The weavers set up empty looms and pretended to work, but in reality they had no wool and weren't making any clothes. The emperor and his court, blinded by the fear of looking foolish, declared they saw the finest, most exquisite fabric they'd ever witnessed. As the "suit" progressed, everyone, from ministers to courtiers, played along, praising the nonexistent clothes.

Some of his people also began to ask the weavers for new clothes for themselves! Even if they couldn't see the cloth, they didn't want to also look stupid, so they put their orders in. Some of them used their life savings to buy the new clothes! Finally, the day of the grand procession arrived. The emperor, stark naked, paraded proudly, basking in the "admiration" of his subjects. Everyone, not knowing what their peers could see and fearing ridicule, continued the charade, until a little child, innocent and unburdened by social pressures, blurted out, "But the emperor has no clothes!"

The truth echoed through the crowd. Shamefaced, the emperor realized he'd been played, and the kingdom learned two valuable lessons: don't be afraid to speak the truth, even if it challenges authority or popular opinion. And second, don't be a follower. The person you may be following might not be setting the right example.

The Emperor's New Clothes

Giving and Getting Feedback Is Hard

When was the last time you gave someone constructive feedback? How was that experience? How did you feel in the process of sharing your insights? Do you remember when you have received feedback that made you uncomfortable?

Giving feedback, especially to someone in a power position over you or to a close friend, can be extremely challenging. It is natural to be more cautious in how you approach that feedback, especially when it is negative in nature. You see the risks involved, even if your feedback is given to help that person improve.

Getting feedback is also a challenge. Are you ready to listen? Do you trust the person giving you that feedback? Do you feel defensive?

Fundamentally, we tend to struggle in both giving and receiving feedback. It makes us uncomfortable. Therefore, we tend to not give feedback. Or if we do, we don't quite give it in a direct, clear manner. You will notice that you tend to soften the message, hoping to make the point but striving to remain comfortable during the conversation. And when you are receiving feedback, your brain wants us to either debate the points or run away. Either way it is hard!

It is so hard in fact, that the child in this folktale was the only one brave enough to point out that the emperor was naked and to give the emperor and others in the town the feedback they needed to hear. The moral of this story emphasizes the value of honest feedback, even when it's difficult.

I don't know about you, but I would hate to walk around in invisible clothes! So maybe getting better at giving and receiving feedback is key to our ability to achieve our goals.

The Neuroscience Behind This Struggle

But why is it so hard to receive feedback? Once again, our brains are the cause and the answer to that question. Our brains have a complex relationship with feedback, particularly negative feedback. Although constructive criticism is incredibly valuable for learning and growth, it can initially trigger a negative response that makes it difficult for people to accept and benefit from that feedback. First, we must understand why we have that initial negative response. Then we can learn to adjust our response to be heathier, thereby truly leveraging the feedback given.

We respond negatively because our brains initially see feedback as a threat. This response is genetically wired into us to help ensure our survival. Here is how that works:

- *The amygdala:* When we receive negative feedback, our amygdala, the brain's "fight-or-flight" center, is activated. This triggers a threat response, as our brains perceive the feedback as a potential danger to your social standing, self-esteem, our relationship status or competence.

- *Fight-or-flight chemicals:* This activation leads to the release of stress hormones like cortisol and adrenaline, which can cause physiological changes like increased heart rate, sweating, and tension. *(I feel this reaction at times when I get constructive feedback from my manager or from people I care about. It feels like heat is rising from my chest to my face!)* These fight-or-flight responses are designed to help us deal with immediate threats, but in the context of feedback, they can lead to defensive behavior and an inability to process the information constructively. Basically, we begin to shut down.

When researching this pattern, I learned from a study by Columbia University neuroscientist Kevin Ochsner that we may only be absorbing 30% of what we are being told. Sometimes, when I get constructive feedback that is difficult to hear, I think I only remember 5% of what was said! Why does that happen?

They call it a *cognitive shut-down,* which is essentially reduced prefrontal cortex activity. This cortex, responsible for executive functions like logic and critical thinking, becomes less active when the amygdala is taken over by the threat response. (I tell my employees it is like our ears are closing. We can only hear so much in this state. We immediately start thinking about our excuses or how we will respond so that we stop actively listening.) This reduces our ability to analyze the feedback rationally, making us more likely to dismiss it or react negatively.

How to Better Absorb Feedback and Grow

Now that you understand why you might view feedback as a threat, how do you shift your mind to be open to feedback? I am always worried that when I get constructive feedback I am retaining the wrong 30%. What wisdom was shared that I missed? How, as a leader, can I help my team better absorb feedback to make them stronger?

Here are some tips to help you view feedback as a tool for growth, rather than as a threat:

- *Shift your mindset:* Approach feedback as an opportunity to learn and improve. Remember, even the best performers can benefit from constructive criticism. None of us is perfect.

- *Listen actively:* Pay close attention to what the person is saying, avoid interrupting, and try to understand their perspective.

- *Be curious, not defensive:* Ask clarifying questions to get a full understanding of the feedback. This shows you're engaged and want to learn more.

- *Acknowledge the effort:* Thank the person for taking the time to provide feedback. It shows you appreciate their input.

- *Consider the source:* Is this someone you trust and respect? Their credibility can influence how you weigh the feedback.

- *Don't take it personally:* Although the feedback is about you, strive to separate your self-worth from your work. Feedback is about the task or behavior, not you as a person.

- *Take time to process:* Don't feel pressured to respond immediately. Take some time to reflect on the feedback before deciding how to proceed.

- *Not all feedback is equal:* Use your judgment to evaluate the feedback. You don't have to follow every suggestion but consider the validity of each point.

(continued)

(continued)

- *Focus on what you can control:* You can't control how feedback is delivered, but you can control your reaction. Choose to see it as a chance to grow.

- *Follow up:* If you decide to implement the feedback, let the person know. This shows that you value their input and are taking action. This also makes them a part of your journey of self-improvement.

    By following these tips, you can reframe feedback as a valuable tool for development, ultimately leading to improved performance and increased satisfaction.

So why all the talk about feedback? Because it is critical to understanding your leadership shadow, which is discussed next.

Your Leadership Shadow

Your *shadow* is a combination of your actions, decisions, and communication style. It is how you make people feel when you are in the room and once you've left that room. It also contributes to how they trust you and engage with you, as well as their willingness to give you constructive feedback along the way should you need or want that input. This shadow is your leadership shadow—it's the unconscious influence or impact you have on those around you. This holds true in business, family, and social settings.

Think about the emperor's shadow. Which of his behaviors or position stopped his people from giving him the feedback he needed to hear? Sometimes, your level at work creates a perceived barrier. Others might feel that there is too much risk to give you negative feedback. Or if it is your friends or family, perhaps they hold back because they don't want to hurt your feelings. Either way, it is important that each of us understands our shadow so that we can realize our goals and have a healthier relationship with those around us. Let's dig into what makes up your shadow.

The following quote by Maya Angelou sums up the impact of your shadow perfectly for me!

> *"I've learned that people will forget what you said, people will forget what you did, but people will never forget how you made them feel."*

How a Leadership Shadow Works

Your leadership shadow isn't created just by what you say, it's the overall message you also send through your behavior, values, and priorities. Ultimately, it's the culture you create as a leader. It's the culture you set at home.

Your team observes your every move, good and bad. They subconsciously pick up on your habits, reactions, and the way you treat others. This in turn shapes their behavior and performance. Like in the story, many in the kingdom purchased their own new clothes even though they couldn't see the cloth for themselves. They followed their leader, assuming that he must be right, that he would look favorably on them as they were not stupid. They were too afraid to question their emperor.

A positive leadership shadow can inspire, motivate, and guide a team to success. A negative shadow can demotivate, create frustration, encourage bad behaviors, and hinder performance. *Watch out: it can even make you buy new clothes that don't exist!*

Feedback Is THE Gift

Without feedback—honest feedback—you are blind. Feedback, regularly requested and given, can help you understand your own shadow. Feedback can reinforce positive attributes that help those around you flourish. It can also give you early warning signs that you are missing something. Feedback—good and bad—makes you smarter! We cannot possibly know everything, so if you listen carefully and with a growth mindset, you will grow and evolve faster than you expected. I also tell my team that even if you don't agree with some of the feedback you are receiving, just knowing how others perceive you is valuable. You get to choose how you want to show up and navigate based on what was shared.

Just think, if the people in the kingdom had given the emperor feedback earlier, he would not have walked naked down the street! Now that would have been a gift.

My Story: Learning About My Shadow

When I was working at Applied Materials, I was leading the people process integration of an Israeli company we had just acquired. At that time, I had three young children. This role required me to travel to various countries to help with this transition and solve the people and process challenges. In this role I was also working with a newly created, large, cross-functional team, so I did not have strong working relationships at first. This assignment was important to the company and to my career. It was complex and we were on a tight timeline.

When I was traveling, I relied on this extended team to assist me in addressing issues as they come up. When all went well, I was able to get home quickly to my family. At other times, I had to extend my trips if the work was not going smoothly. During those times, I struggled. I wanted to be home with my young family.

I clearly remember one trip that was extended when I was in Singapore, a long way from home. I noticed that 10 employees took longer to respond than normal. When they finally responded, their responses were short. They didn't appear to take the initiative to help close the problem. I didn't see them taking any extra steps to move the ball forward. I was getting frustrated. I needed help. What made it worse was that I was sure that my frustration showed in my voice and in my written emails.

That week, after closing out a few issues, I kept coming back to the question—what was going on? I realized that these employees didn't work in the same department as each other. Some were in different physical locations. Bottom line—they didn't know each other. The only common element was me. Ugh.

I had to be the problem.

(continued)

The Emperor's New Clothes

(continued)

What was I doing wrong? I did not know. I didn't have a clue. I never asked for feedback. That wasn't my strength.

After I got home, I sought a coach to help me navigate this situation. I wanted to fix this problem or, at the very least, prevent it from happening again. My coach, Denise, was fabulous. I trusted her. She focused on executive leadership. I asked for help to solicit feedback from these individuals. She asked me if I wanted to do a full 360 evaluation to get a broader view of me, getting feedback from my manager, others on my team, and internal customers. I said no. I wanted to focus on where I seemed to be going wrong.

(On writing this book, I noticed that I did not make it a point to meet with my coworkers individually to seek their feedback directly. Perhaps it was my concern with my ability to not get defensive, or the fact I thought it would be easier for them to be more candid to a stranger? In the end, I realized I was probably nervous about the feedback. Would I be able to truly hear what they had to say? It mattered to me. I was aware that what I would hear, needed to hear, would be hard. I needed help so that I would truly understand the challenges I was facing. An accountability partner—my coach— would work with me to ensure I truly learned the lesson I needed to learn.)

I remember the day I got the feedback summary. I remember where I was in the East Bay in Northern

California, where I sat. I was in a booth, the window at my back, in a loud restaurant. It was sunny. It felt like the day was too bright for a day when I knew I would hear hard things.

Denise took me to a Mexican restaurant near my office. While we were sitting there looking at the menus, she cut to the chase. "Pat, the feedback is consistent. It is important that you really absorb this feedback and then we can plan how best to address the next steps. Are you ready to listen?"

I could feel my body heating up and getting a bit clammy. Already I was feeling anxious and defensive, and she hadn't even given me the feedback yet! I took a deep breath and reminded myself that I asked for these insights. It was important. I had to keep my ears open.

Next, she dug into the key themes. I was ready to learn about my shadow.

"Everyone was surprised you asked for their feedback but were very willing to participate. In general, they don't know you and you don't know them outside of their responsibilities. You seemed to not appreciate their work or their work efforts. When you are in the office with them, you eat lunch by yourself. In the mornings you walk past them without checking in to see how they are doing. When the teams invite you to social hours after work, you never show up. Their assumption is that you don't like them or respect their work and are only motivated to achieve your goals."

(continued)

The Emperor's New Clothes

(continued)

My Reaction Was Normal: I Was Ashamed and Hurt

I was stunned. While absorbing this quick but brutal feedback, I realized that my feelings were also hurt. My initial response that came to my head were excuses. Or to say they misread me. They were wrong. It wasn't my intent to come across that way. In the end, it didn't matter. Their perception was their reality. My leadership shadow for them was ugly. Sitting in their space, examining our various interactions, they were right.

Denise asked me why they saw me that way when others did not? What were the missing pieces or the different behaviors that possibly led to this experience?

I explained that I'm an introvert. Eating by myself is a way to get back some energy, recharge, and sift through my thoughts. I was also a new mom, still breast feeding, so when they invited me out after work hours, I was rushing home to be with my babies. And when I was traveling and frustrated that they didn't get the right work done, or done completely, I was short with them. I just demanded more. I wanted to get home. My breast milk that I stored for when I was traveling was running out. I was missing my family. Denise just listened.

Learning to Share Who I Am and My Values

After a pause, Denise kindly asked me if I shared any of that information with these 10 individuals. If not, why not? My quick response was that it wasn't their business. It was personal. Why would they care?

I could tell by Denise's face that I answered incorrectly. She would raise this one eyebrow, and I knew I was off base somehow.

It was then that she talked about the power of the leader. She described the shadow we create for others and that the shadow could be seen differently by different people depending on our interactions with them. This group of individuals did not see me the way I wanted to be seen. They did not know who I was nor I them. Denise coached me to realize that the team needed to know me. They deserved to know me, my values, the context for my decisions, and my struggles. Once they are ready and willing, I should strive to get to know them.

They needed to know these elements to better support me and each other. They did not want to follow me blindly. They believed that I did not respect them, and they felt our values were not aligned. I had let them down.

Denise recommended that I meet with two of the individuals, thanking them for their feedback and striving to change my shadow. Make it a healthy shadow for them. My homework was to pick two.

Intentionality with My Shadow

The next day, after a long night, I picked all 10 to engage with and strive to make right. I called Denise and shared my goal. She asked me why all 10? My response:

Simply because I owe all of them my sincere apology. I owe them my gratitude for providing this

(continued)

105

(continued)

> *feedback. Going forward, I will be better because
> of this feedback. I owe them a chance to get to
> know me and I them. You see, what I realized is
> that when I got frustrated with their work, I forgot
> to treat them with kindness and respect. They did
> work hard but the challenges were complex, and
> they didn't know the impact of me being away
> from home even longer. When I ate by myself, or
> did not attend happy hour events, I thought that
> they wouldn't notice or care. I was wrong.*

That next week I scheduled two meetings a day. I was vulnerable, honest, listened more, asked more questions to truly understand, and expressed gratitude for their feedback. I shared with them what I shared with Denise. I never was that open with my coworkers prior to those sessions. I ended each meeting with a request to reboot. To give them permission to provide real-time feedback to me when I am showing my ugly shadow. They deserved to be treated beautifully, even when we are disagreeing or giving constructive feedback.

Grateful for the Lesson!

I wish I had learned this lesson earlier. Some of those initial meetings were tough. Some pushed me even further and shared more concerns, where others were surprised and grateful for the apology and the reboot. Every session was exhausting. It was emotional. Several times, I sat in the parking lot afterwards and just reflected—or cried.

To lead others means to give more of ourselves. To be more transparent and vulnerable than we expect. I needed to know the humans, not just their role and title. They also had unique needs, challenges, and strengths that I was not aware of until those fateful meetings. Trust would only come once I became more open, authentic, and vulnerable.

I'm grateful for that lesson and have respected the impact of my shadow from that point forward. I have shared with my teams many years later that every employee deserves to be treated beautifully. Even when delivering tough messages, you can and should treat everyone with respect, kindness, and care. I also deserve to be treated beautifully. This foundational belief has become a cornerstone of my personal scorecard.

With Denise's wisdom and my commitment to a healthier shadow, we built a stronger relationship across the broader teams. As a result of our stronger bonds, connection to each other, and our values, we became a stronger and more effective team. We crushed our deliverables and had fun doing it. I was honored that after that project, many followed me to future roles and opportunities.

I am forever grateful for their feedback. Today my shadow is much different. I seek feedback regularly, so I don't miss something or create new bad habits. I also strive to be consistently me, at home, in the office, meeting strangers, or hanging out with friends. Having this level of consistency helps remind me to always be my best self, to not take others for granted, and to show appreciation and love regularly.

Work Example: Teaching the Shadow Lesson

Recently, I was teaching a few hundred senior leaders about the leadership shadow concept. Many had never heard of this before. We shared examples, large and small, that could affect one's shadow. One example that hit home was when one senior leader canceled the one-on-one meetings with their direct report on a regular basis. They often spoke, so the senior leader believed that they were in sync and thought that by canceling the one-on-one meetings, the manager was giving the employee the gift of time. They believed they were demonstrating trust by canceling those meetings.

The employee did not see the meeting cancellations in a positive light. They saw their leader cancel a meeting without any context or notice. The employee felt that their manager didn't respect their time and did not consider the fact that they had created a report to share with their manager. The employee was left feeling underappreciated, not respected, and less engaged as a result. I asked the audience the following:

- *Are you aware of your shadow's influence?* Perhaps, if you are modeling bad behaviors, you could be creating blind conformity that leads to absurd or bad situations. In the folktale, folks in the kingdom were buying invisible clothes to copy the emperor so they would not appear stupid. In some companies, I have seen employees take on the bad habits of their managers. What habits are you giving to others?

- *Who speaks the truth to you?* Give and seek feedback with honesty and hopefully with compassion. Independent thinking and courage are also essential.

The child in this fable dared to speak the truth and, with that statement, made others realize their own shortcomings.

To drive the point home, I asked, "How many of you canceled a meeting with one of your employees for similar reasons and in similar fashion?" Many hands were raised. This created a great conversation at each table about how small acts could shape perceptions. They were so energized with this conversation that they kept giving each other additional examples of behaviors that could be interpreted incorrectly. Being late to meetings, looking at their phones during a one-on-one meeting, drinking a bit too much at business functions, or even walking by without saying hello. They got the point!

The leaders wanted to know their shadows. I was thrilled. As a head of HR, having leaders who want to know and then adjust their shadows to create a healthier team feels amazing!

Reflection: Determining Your Leadership Shadow

Take a moment and reflect on your habits at work. What messages are you inadvertently sending? What behaviors are acceptable? What feedback do you solicit from your team?

In addition, what you see—even if it's poor behavior—might become your norm. If my leader drinks a lot at work functions, I can, too. Being late to meetings becomes the norm. I am sure you have other examples. With that said, what behaviors do you see around you or from your leadership that may be creating an unhealthy shadow for the organization?

Having the Courage to Speak Up

One of my managers used to put his feet on his desk in front of where I was sitting while he was looking at his computer when we were having our one-on-one meeting. He would be like that when I walked in, and he did not change his behavior once I began sharing my agenda items. Clearly, I felt that I was not his priority. His behavior made me feel less valued and disrespected. However, I was not sure he was aware of his leadership shadow. I decided to test this hypothesis. One day when he continued to do this, I stopped talking and just sat there. He asked me after a few minutes why I wasn't chatting while he was still looking at his computer. I said that I was waiting to get his full attention as I believed my work and the topics I wanted to share mattered. That got his attention. He put his feet down, turned toward me, and we began. After that time, in my one-on-one meetings with him, he would adjust his body language and give me his full attention. He became more aware of his shadow.

Taking that stand and giving him that feedback was hard. Did you know that giving feedback is just as hard as receiving feedback? Yup! When we give feedback to someone, we tend to soften the message so we don't hurt their feelings. We don't want to damage our relationship with that person, or we are afraid of their reaction.

Here are some simple tips for giving constructive feedback that I encourage you to follow if you want your wisdom to be heard:

- *Start with a positive:* Acknowledge their effort or strength before diving into areas for improvement.

- *Focus on specifics:* Instead of saying "your presentation needs work," for example, say "you need to add data to support your arguments."

- *Focus on the behavior, not on the person:* "The meeting starts at 10 a.m., and we all need to be on time. Being late causes us to rush through the agenda items."

- *Be open to a two-way conversation:* Feedback is a dialogue. You may learn how best to support someone by listening.

- *Choose the right place and time:* Giving feedback in public is likely to embarrass that person and lower their capacity to listen and learn.

In Summary: Being Aware of Your Shadow

The moral of the emperor's story is the danger of conformity and social pressure. The people in the story are afraid to speak up against the emperor's nonexistent clothes because they fear his position of power. This highlights the dangers of blindly following the crowd and not trusting your own judgment.

Be aware of your shadow, personally and professionally. Remember, your leadership shadow is always present, whether you're aware of it or not. By reflecting on your actions and seeking feedback, you can consciously shape your shadow and create a positive influence on your team, community, and organization.

So where is your shadow? What shape is it? Can you see all of it? Are you willing to work to share your shadow into a healthier shape? And most important, are you creating the safe space so others can give you the feedback you need so you are not naked like the emperor?

Practice seeking and giving feedback. Feedback is the gift you need so you don't walk around naked! Create psychological safety and be sincere when asking for feedback. Thank the person who gave you that feedback! Their feedback might be the key to your future success! Giving and getting feedback is a muscle we must all work on. I am still actively working on it. As I said at the beginning of this chapter, getting and giving feedback is hard. I am perfectly imperfect. However, with feedback received along your journey, you can course correct early, thereby adjusting bad habits before your shadow runs away from you.

Continue with me on this journey of self-discovery. In Chapter 7, you have the opportunity to meet the crow. The crow happens to be one of my favorite stories of all. He will guide you on how to evolve and strengthen your shadow beyond your expectations by leveraging creativity and facing constraints that are inevitable during every journey.

The Crow and the Pitcher

Unlocking the Creativity of Constraints

The Crow and the Pitcher

Unlocking the Creativity of Constraints

Once upon a time, on a hot, sunny day, a crow was flying around looking for water. He was very thirsty, but he couldn't find any water. He looked high and low until finally he came across a large ceramic pitcher with water in it. But the water was too far down for him to reach.

The crow tried many ways to get to the water. He tried to tip the pitcher over, but it was too heavy. He tried to move a stick under the pitcher to tilt it, but he couldn't squeeze the stick under the heavy pitcher. Then he tried to get his beak deep into the pitcher, but the neck of the pitcher was too narrow to fit his whole head.

The crow was starting to give up hope, but then he had a new idea. He looked around and beside the sticks, he saw pebbles and rocks. The crow began to pick up pebbles and drop them into the pitcher. One by one, the pebbles filled up the pitcher, and the water level slowly rose. Finally, after a while, the water was high enough for the crow to reach. He was so happy! He could quench his thirst at last.

The Influence of Constraints

I have been inspired by this Aesop's fable because the moral of this story reminds me of overcoming obstacles through grit, believing in oneself, and creativity. The solution of putting pebbles into the pitcher was something that would never have occurred to me. At least, not at first. That creativity drew me in. It is a daily reminder and inspiration for me when I feel self-doubt. It lets me believe that there is always a solution to a problem; I just have to find it.

Initially, I thought that being an introvert and having learning differences were insurmountable obstacles—constraints on my ability to achieve my dreams. Both attributes are part of me and cannot be changed. But I learned that these attrib-utes were also gifts that I needed to unwrap. As I shared previously, I never even imagined writing a book! As you know, I love to tell a good story, so what held me back? It was the story in my head. A false constraint. More on that concept in a minute.

So why did I choose this Aesop's fable? "The Crow and the Pitcher" is a simple tale that imparts valuable lessons about resourcefulness and perseverance, and it highlights the creativity that emerges through constraints. As I've done with the other stories, I have made this one a bit of my own and have embraced its message about how people approach challenges or, better yet, perceive constraints in our lives. The story is a reminder to persevere. To "sit with a problem" so you can come up with potential solutions.

When I was younger, I gave up too quickly. I didn't sit with the problem, I ran away from it. I enabled self-doubt and others' perceived constraints of me to guide how I reacted to life's challenges. These perceived constraints allowed me to believe, even into adulthood, that writing a book was out of reach. To put oneself out there in the world, in a very personal way—and do it authentically— was an out of reach goal. But then, I learned about the power of *yet* and the theory of constraints. Without those two concepts, I could never have written this book. I did not write my first long post on LinkedIn until I was in my 50s.

From a business leadership perspective, it was easier for me to apply the theory of constraints with my teams. I shared with them the theory of false constraints and encouraged the team to apply this approach, intentionally embedding it into our thinking and ensuring that we were being creative in our problem-solving. Now, mind you, the planner in me would much rather operate under the auspices of a false constraint, than find myself reacting to a real one. That's because facing constraints as they come up often means finding solutions with limited time and resources. By anticipating potential constraints, it basically becomes a proactive approach versus a reactive one.

A Breakdown of Constraints

There are essentially three types of constraints in my way of thinking:

- *False constraints*, which we place in front of us when faced with challenges or changes that make us uncomfortable. These are typically blocks we throw up without real data.
- *"Proactive" creative constraints*, whereby we place self-imposed constraints to push our thinking to be more creative and pragmatic. I call these *proactive creative constraints* because they push us to be more innovative in finding solutions.
- *Real constraints* that we face in life, such as time, money, or perhaps skills that limit our choices.

False Constraints

When you think about false constraints, what comes to mind? These constraints are self-imposed (sometimes influenced by others). They can be based on assumptions, outdated beliefs, or fear of change, and they can significantly hinder progress and innovation. They hold many people

117

back when in problem-solving mode or when brainstorming potential opportunities.

This theory of false constraints generally refers to the idea that you often limit yourself or your organization by *accepting perceived constraints* that aren't true or necessary. If you believe that false constraint, you are less empowered, have lower confidence, and are quieter in the discussion. You shrink.

For me, my learning challenges throughout my early educational experience, the belief that I was not smart enough, and being an introvert were the mantras in my head that became false constraints. Many of these constraints are influenced by others around us and the words they use to describe us. If we are not careful, we will also see ourselves through those lenses. For example, leaders are expected to be extroverted. That was typically seen as a strength. Being quieter is seen as less confident or perhaps lacking an ability to influence. I thankfully shed those false constraints, but those imposter syndrome/false constraint beliefs creep up on my shoulders every now and then and need to be batted down!

Proactive Creative Constraints

What happens if we purposefully put false constraints into our problem-solving? What does that unleash? This practice is what I call *proactive creative constraints*. It is inserting potential false constraints into the narrative to help stimulate problem-solving and increase agility. For example, think about an economic downturn, a loss of a key customer, a rejected loan, a key employee quitting, or even a significant reduction in revenue. Think about the key variables in your planning. Ones that, if they went wrong, would have a significant negative impact on your results or your ability to achieve your goals on time. Those areas are excellent targets to apply potential constraints.

By proactively applying these false constraints before a real problem emerges, you can unlock the creativity of the team. You will begin to anticipate these potential future challenges and the risks associated with each one and feel more confident as you create your final plans. By being proactive, you can take the time needed to include other stakeholders earlier, create more robust solutions with greater buy-in, and have clarity of prioritization should one of these events occur.

Real Constraints

Real constraints are part of everyday life. We need or should address them head on. But, when we are creating programs, determining a business strategy, or even setting up an annual budget, there is benefit to breaking down false constraints and in some cases introducing proactive creative constraints to ensure our best thinking. In fact, when we learn to navigate both false and creative constraints, our ability to address life's real constraints become easier.

The Process: Applying Creative Constraints at Work

You can try this at work for any key initiative. The proactive approach to creative constraints is literally putting restrictions on resources—money, people, time, competitive market threats—to begin problem-solving the what-if scenarios now. Be aware that you are also slowing down and creating friction at the front end of this process to ensure you have a more robust solution and alternative paths should real constraints emerge later. This is the fun part.

After the team proposes constraints and their solutions, I ask them to define the cost of yes as it relates to their proposed solutions. This flushes out the impact of that decision—the potential unintended impact of these choices on key stakeholders, time, cost, resources, and prioritization of work that the team might be navigating. So, if we shorten the time to market, the cost of yes might be delaying another product or program. Knowing how to determine these trade-offs is key to leading a highly efficient and effective organization.

You can also do this same analysis with the cost of no. If you say no to a project or opportunity, what could be the downstream impact of that decision? Rest assured that whether you say yes or no, there is opportunity cost.

Opportunity cost is basically the trade-off you make when you choose one thing over another. It is the loss of the thing you give up by making a different choice. For example, let's say you decide to see a movie instead of studying for an exam. The opportunity cost of seeing the movie is the good grade you might have gotten if you had studied. You can't have both the fun of the movie and the good grade, so you have to give something up. Every decision involves giving up something else.

This process works extremely well when applied to annual planning or when we do multiyear strategy sessions. When you do this exercise in your organization, or when attempting to pursue a large opportunity, you'll feel more confident in your ultimate strategies. Without thinking about constraints, it is too easy to create an organization that is bloated and inefficient or a product that is too expensive to produce profitably at scale. It also helps you navigate the inevitable trade-offs you must make each day.

Regarding the annual budget exercises, I guide my team to model their plans with a significantly reduced budget, say a 20% cut, to ensure we are thinking optimally about our resources. This forces clear prioritization and focus. Once we have pushed hard enough, we can determine the best and highest leverage of the resources we are given. We also have a plan B or even a plan C in case we are asked to reduce spending later to adjust for P&L pressures.

Using this process, not only does the team gain clarity but it also gives the team a sense of empowerment, control, and a bit of confidence that they have a few paths to take should real constraints come their way. We can pivot quickly and feel strong about our course of actions.

Learning how to adapt, to be creative, is key to leading through constraints. They prepare us for when real constraints pop up into our lives—like COVID-19.

Example: The Real Constraints of COVID-19

When COVID-19 spread across the globe, the world stopped and collectively we all had to figure a bunch of things out. Implementing global IT systems or doing product innovation was tackled with an completely remote workforce! The list of things that were affected by COVID-19 is endless, or at least it felt that way to me. We sent everyone home in March 2020, believing COVID-19 was only a several-week problem. A hiccup on our path—perhaps a short-term constraint even? My team had to onboard dozens of new hires over that initial period. Typically, we flew folks to corporate or a local office to conduct in person orientation. That wasn't going to happen. And we didn't have everything digital. We quickly realized our dilemma.

We, like most companies, pulled together a working team to determine—given our new constraints—how to onboard and ramp up our new talent. We did not want to delay hire dates, waiting for COVID-19 to end. (Can you believe we actually thought that was an option?) This cross-functional team made up of IT folks, human resources (HR) business partners, recruiters, event planners, and trainers came up with amazing ways to host our sessions fully remote. They converted information to digital format quickly—prioritizing what was necessary versus nice to have—and became very focused on the intent of the onboarding process. In fact, through their diligence, prioritization, and creativity, many of those solutions remain today. That constraint—the inability to travel/meet in person—created a better way to hire/ramp up new hires and saved the company money. We would never have created a program like this without the constraint of COVID-19. I wonder what else we might be missing if we don't put false constraints in our way from time to time?

Reflection: Exploring Your Constraints

You can leverage your Goldilocks framework to help guide you with this reflection:

- Do you have a false constraint bouncing around inside your head that pertains to a career or goal aspiration? (For example, do you believe that being an introvert will stop you from being an amazing leader?)

- Do your false constraints inhibit your ability to evolve your leadership shadow into how you want it to be? (Does being an introvert lower your confidence in your ability to network or influence your organization?)

- Have you heard others apply constraints relating to you? Maybe they think that you can't be a leader unless you are always networking and making small talk with the customers and employees. That when you are quiet, you are not as competent.

- Have you reflected on what feels true to who you are versus how others perceive you? (For example, as an introvert, you have an ability to develop strong, trusting relationships. You connect deeply with those around you, spending time to know who they are and their needs. Isn't that a strength to be embraced as a leader?)

It is up to each of us to unpack false statements, digest what is truly us, and imagine a world where we can navigate life. We can achieve our career and life objectives by overcoming creatively real constraints or by throwing away labels or constraints that others have given to us.

The Crow and the Pitcher

My Original False Constraint

Early in my life, due to my struggles and poor grades in math, spelling, and writing, I believed I was not smart. My family either reinforced that assessment or thought I didn't have the work ethic to learn. My early education teachers also accepted that belief and tailored some of my assignments to be easier and less challenging. Therefore, I lost opportunities to learn and grow. These false constraints continued in high school, where I chose not to seek challenging courses. Due to this lack of confidence, I didn't believe I could go to a prestigious college, so I never applied. I just followed my brother to a local college in Louisiana. Basically, I accepted those false constraints as my own.

When I discovered I was dyslexic in college, that newfound awareness squelched that internal false narrative of being lazy or not smart. The false constraint was gone. I was now free to dream and explore possibilities that were never before on my horizon line.

Addressing False Constraint Narratives

It is important for leaders to be able to identify when they or their teams are operating in a false constraint mindset. You will bump into such a mindset during times of change or when attempting to launch a huge initiative. This is normal. Our first instinct is to protect ourselves from failure. It is therefore up to you, as the leader, to sense this challenge and address it early and head on.

You can also apply this approach to your children, too! I found it incredibly powerful to catch myself, my young adult children, or my team in the beginning of this phase so we can quickly pivot and make it a positive approach with better outcomes. When my oldest son was in high school, he carried a false constraint that he also wasn't smart. He excelled at sports, but not academically. Some friends reinforced the "dumb jock" persona. As a parent, I was frustrated, as I did not believe in his constraints.

When he was a junior, he decided he wanted to go to college. It was his goal. Not a goal given to him by his parents. He understood that to get accepted he needed better grades. Then he focused. He was motivated. He buckled down and put in the effort, and he excelled. He broke away from his own false constraints and became more confident. When he went on to college and perhaps had a low grade or two, he took accountability for not putting in the effort versus not having the ability to perform well. That made me happy! This evolution of accountability and self-confidence will continue to guide him well in life.

Recognizing the False Signals

The first step is to recognize and challenge assumptions about what is possible or impossible. This requires critical thinking and a willingness to question the status quo. I carefully listen to the team, my children, or my customers to see if they are using language that lets me know that they are self-limiting and putting in place false constraints on any potential future actions.

It is important to ask questions at this stage. Be sure you can echo back clearly what you are hearing so that others can see themselves and their false constraints in your summary.

Listen to the words you and your team uses to help identify when a false restrictive constraint is being perceived:

- Time constraints ("We/I don't have enough time to do that.")
- Resource constraints ("We/I don't have the budget for that.")
- Capability constraints ("We/I don't have the skills to do that.")
- Procedural constraints ("That's not how we do things here.")

Shifting Away from False Constraints

To move away from false constraints, follow these steps:

- *Change your mindset:* Begin to pivot by reframing the false challenges and putting on your growth mindset hat. Instead of viewing constraints as fixed barriers, reframe them as problems to be solved or opportunities for creativity. You just haven't solved this particular problem *yet.*
- *Break down barriers:* Once you have identified the false constraints, explore ways to overcome them. This might involve the following:
  - Rethinking priorities
  - Challenging traditional approaches

- Fostering innovation and experimentation
- Seeking external expertise (cocreation with others who have walked similar paths)
- *Unlock the potential:* By breaking free from false constraints, individuals and organizations can tap into hidden potential, achieve greater success, and drive innovation.

> *Growth mindset* is the idea that abilities can be developed. To have a growth mindset, you must be receptive to feedback, learn from your experiences, and refine your strategies as circumstances evolve. If you haven't read Carol Dweck's work on mindset (*Mindset: The New Psychology of Success* [Ballantine Books, 2013]), I highly suggest you do!

By recognizing and addressing false constraints, individuals and organizations can unlock new possibilities, build more skills, and achieve greater success.

The Power of *Yet*—Unlocking Constraints

This fable also reminded me of the power of a growth mindset. For me, it's a way to view life and problems from an optimistic point of view. Just because you have not faced a problem before, or your initial response did not create a desirable solution, don't give up. You just realize that you haven't solved the problem yet. The crow approached his problem from several different directions. He knew that he must get water and soon. The pitcher had water; he just needed to get to it. He believed in himself, did not give up, and ultimately figured out that if he couldn't get down to the water, the water had to get to him.

My Yet Moment

When I worked at Applied Materials, I pivoted out of a director of HR role and took on a new role as the business readiness lead for a company-wide Oracle implementation. My key partner was the technical lead and we both reported to a senior executive sponsor. I had never led a large change management effort in the past at this scale and complexity. My goal was to get the organization ready for this transformation: technology and process changes. I had many resources available to me to support this pivotal role. I made many mistakes. And I grew.

In my first business readiness meeting with the top senior leaders of the company, I failed. My data was right. My approach was wrong. I was so focused on my data, showing how smart my team and I were, that I forgot our purpose: getting the business ready for this big change. As a result, our business readiness dashboard reflected red and yellow status across all four divisions. The division leaders were upset. I let them down and it was clear I was losing their trust.

I had focused on showing them that I knew the data, but I did not focus on the necessary action plans to get them to yellow or green. The meeting was going so poorly that Jim Morgan, the CEO at the time, suggested that I end the meeting early and return when I felt we were back on track. I agreed. Thanks to my manager, I learned how to pick myself up after that meeting, to own that mistake, and course correct appropriately. I learned how to ask for help and stay curious so that we could provide the best solutions. I learned how to lead a cross-functional team across the globe and come out stronger, wiser, and with more friends.

I hadn't done that type of program yet . . . but then I did. I did it with amazingly talented coworkers, a sponsor who challenged my false constraints, and a peer who made me feel like I could do anything. This program, which took approximately two years to complete, is one of my proudest accomplishments, not because I helped implement an Oracle ERP system but because I faced my constraints and I grew.

Now I run toward my next yet moment.

In Summary: Facing Your Constraints

Ultimately the crow faced his constraints and figured out a way to drink the much needed water. Like him, I have navigated false and real constraints in my life. What I've learned is that I grow the most when I am challenged. I've become more creative in my approach and have a deeper sense of accomplishment once I've achieved my yet goals. Life continues to be unpredictable, and I'm sure I will have many more challenges ahead.

Here are some key takeaways from the crow's experience:

- *The theory of constraints:* This theory stimulates out-of-the-box thinking, resourcefulness, and creativity. If you are determined and don't give up, you can overcome any obstacle. Effective leaders can analyze situations from different perspectives, identify unconventional solutions, and implement strategies that break free from established norms.

- *Perseverance and determination:* Despite initial setbacks, the crow didn't succumb to frustration or act like a victim but continued to experiment and devise new approaches until he succeeded. This resilience is a crucial trait for all of us, enabling us to navigate challenges and achieve long-term goals.

- *Having a growth mindset:* As the crow fills the pitcher with pebbles, he continuously adapted his actions based on the changing water level. This adaptability highlights the importance of continuous learning and flexibility. Leaders must be receptive to feedback, learn from their experiences, and refine their strategies as circumstances evolve.

> Innovative problem-solving get even stronger when you seek others to create solutions with you. You also get broader buy-in on the solutions.

By emulating the crow's resourcefulness, perseverance, and problem-solving abilities, you can navigate challenges with an open mind, inspire others, and achieve remark-able success in your endeavors. I also encourage you to embrace challenges, perceive constraints as a gift of learn-ing, and embrace your creativity. Although my learning path has been hard at times, I've discovered that being dyslexic has made me more creative in how I approach problems. I also have more resilience and am more com-passionate with my teams and individuals who learn dif-ferently or face their own unique challenges. Last but not least, I've become more confident because of all I have been able to accomplish by experiencing my yet moments.

Are you ready for your next yet growth moment? In Chapter 8, you meet my friend the frog. He exemplifies the impact of knowing our values and embracing them as we jump toward our next yet moment. I hope you enjoy him as much as I do!

The Frog in Boiling Water
Living a Values-Led Life

*O*nce upon a time there was a frog living by a pond, but he was very cold. His other frog friends didn't understand why he was so cold. They were just fine jumping in and out of the pond and sunning themselves in the sunlight.

One day, a farmer came by, saw the frog shivering, and offered to warm him up. Mr. Frog was happy with that offer! So, the farmer took him home and put the frog in a pot of tepid water. Mr. Frog was very happy to get warmed up and began to swim around a bit. Slowly he closed his eyes and took a nap in the warm water.

The farmer, noticing that the frog was so relaxed, started to heat the water up even more. Maybe he thought he might have frog for dinner? The water temperature kept increasing gradually over time. At one point the frog woke up a bit drowsy due to being so warm and asked the farmer about the temperature of the water. "Farmer, I am enjoying this relaxing bath, but it seems a bit warm don't you think?" The farmer replied "Mr. Frog, the warm water is meant to relax you and make you happy. Just close your eyes a bit longer and you will be just fine. You will get use to the heat." The frog had a nagging feeling that things weren't right, but he decided to ignore it and trust the farmer.

Shortly thereafter, the frog reopened his eyes and was very weak. He realized the water was very hot and he was at risk of being boiled alive! At that point, he gathered all of his strength, leapt out of the water, and jumped all the way home back to the pond with his friends and family. He embraced both the cold of the pond and the warmth of the sun, never taking the heat or cold for granted.

The Frog in Boiling Water

Tapping into Values to Avoid the Boiling Water

This story is not a fable but rather a metaphor, yet I find the lessons in this story to be profound. I am drawn to this story because I think about how, if you stay in a situation that gets progressively worse over time, would you notice it in time to get out unharmed? Would your inner moral compass and values nudge you that something was heading in the wrong direction? I've seen individuals lose their way, and I've seen others who picked up on the clues, saw the symptoms that didn't fit them, and leapt to a better lily pad, so to speak.

Leaping to a better lily pad doesn't just refer to potentially changing your job or leaving your company. This metaphor could also be taking a leap in faith—embracing a new perspective, or reshaping the lily pad you are on to make it healthier. It is about taking action to align your situation with your values.

Although many have heard this metaphor, some folks may cringe when they hear it, as in most versions, the frog dies. Truth be told, a frog would never behave this way in real life. However, I believe the story continues to be widely told because of its practical wisdom, simple storyline, and wide applications.

> You will note that I wrote my own ending so that the frog would live. I love an ending where all the characters live happily ever after. So in practical terms, I took a metaphor and turned it into a fable. A fable that I love to share.

The Origin/Evolution of the Frog Story

Although widely known, no one is clear on its origin. This concept appears in various forms throughout history, making it difficult to pinpoint a single origin story. Being intrigued, I dug in a bit more:

- *Science experiments (seems logical but wow!):* Some scientific experiments were conducted in the nineteenth century to explore animal reflexes, but they focused on observing immediate reactions to sudden temperature changes, not gradual increases.

- *Metaphorical evolution:* The "frog in boiling water" as a metaphor gained traction in the twentieth century, likely influenced by these scientific observations. You can see references to this story when people illustrate the dangers of complacency and gradual environmental changes.

- *It's popular:* Most people know this story and its lessons. Several folks I chatted with didn't like the version where the frog died in the boiling water. Thank goodness I changed the ending!

What I found fascinating was that this metaphor has been applied to various situations to help the audience realize the gradual changes occurring around them. In fact, this is exactly why I leverage this metaphor when I coach. Examples include the following:

- *Personal growth (the main lesson I took away):* You might not realize you've fallen into bad habits or negative patterns until they significantly affect your life.

Remember the Emperor's New Clothes from Chapter 6? The value of getting honest feedback is critical. This can also work the other way—you have been strengthening certain skills over time, but you just don't see them unless you step back a bit.

- *Social issues:* Gradual erosion of rights or freedoms can go unnoticed until it's too late to rectify. You see this across the world in every culture.

The Power of a Simple Story

What also makes this metaphor so compelling are the various lessons in this simple story. When I reference this story, nearly everyone I am coaching can relate to a point I am making. How I love this shortcut to understanding!

The frog's story emphasizes the impact of values in our life and our life choices. Are your values clear to you? When in conflict, would you address the problem head on? How long would you wait to face it? Would you be willing to work to make it better aligned to your values?

I have learned that people tend to underestimate the impact or strain on their values when dealing with "boiling water" situations (e.g. the company, the team you work with, or the friends you are keeping). This ties directly to the Goldilocks framework. I have found that as you age and have more life experiences, your values sharpen and become clearer to you. You know when and how best to leap! You can see the signals sooner when something isn't a right fit or the water temperature is getting too high.

The Value of Values

Let's explore how our values play a role in how we respond to the "boiling water" around us. Hint: They should play a big role!

Have you ever worked at a company or as part of a team where you didn't feel like you quite fit in? Did you reflect on why you felt that way? I feel like I don't belong when my values don't line up with the company or team, or when something is "off" with my relationship with my boss or peer. It is usually a gradual awareness that happens over weeks, months, or in some cases years.

When I reflect on those moments, it came down to my values not being aligned with my peers, my boss, or the overall company culture. Some of these situations were slight differences in how people approached each other or business decisions. Some were more significant and therefore easier to spot. At times like that, it required a review of my Goldilocks framework to determine how I was feeling aligned with my values and motivators.

Each of those experiences helped me realize just how my values drive my actions. Yes, motivators matter, but at a foundational level, we want to work with and be surrounded by individuals who have similar values. If we are unclear on our values, then we may not notice the water temperature increasing, or even perhaps boiling, until it is too late.

My Story: Time to Leap

Earlier in my career, I was frustrated with my manager. It felt like we weren't on the same Page particularly regarding fairness within the team. I noticed that he wasn't treating everyone equitably, despite acknowledging me as a top performer. Although these special considerations bothered me, I hesitated to address it. I simply wasn't sure how to bring it up without feeling awkward.

During our annual review, I finally decided to share my observations and concerns about a lack of fairness. I mentioned how certain team members received perks not offered to everyone whether they achieved or exceeded their goals. Unfortunately, my manager became defensive. (Remember how hard it is to receive feedback?) He justified his actions and implied that I should accept things as they were, even suggesting that this was the best job I could find. This left me feeling unheard and disrespected. My values of respect and fairness clearly weren't aligning with his approach.

The next day, I accepted another role from another company that had been interested in me for a while. My manager was surprised I had taken a leap.

Looking back with the benefit of experience, I realize I should have spoken up sooner. Open communication could have enabled us to address my concerns and find a solution. However, my younger self was frustrated and saw a clear misalignment with my values. So, I left.

This job change proved to be a valuable learning experience. I held true to my values, but it also highlighted the importance of trying to improve a situation before making a drastic jump. In my zeal, I leapt to a new lily pad without exploring all of my options. Thankfully, that new opportunity propelled my career forward.

Interestingly, after some time, I reconnected with my old boss. Our conversations, fueled by reflection, helped us both grow. He apologized, and I gained valuable insight into myself. I learned the importance of timely communication, how to give constructive feedback, and the need to check my ego before making rash decisions. Not a bad lesson to learn!

Knowing when to leap is never easy, especially when you're deciding when to leave a job. Sometimes the timing isn't right. Earlier in my career, I wrestled with the decision of staying to further my career or leaving due to a values clash. Sometimes, I hung on for specific goals or simply because I needed a steady paycheck. (I needed to pay my rent!) In other cases, I tried to change the work environment (my metaphorical lily pad!). Success wasn't guaranteed, and when my efforts failed, I moved on. But when I succeeded, I stayed.

The key, I've learned, is to assess the situation (how hot is that water?) and then choose the path that best aligns with my values. My values remain my guiding light and temperature gauge, helping me navigate the ever-changing landscape of my career.

Value Misalignment Can Be Subtle

Living with your values misaligned can have a subtle yet potent effect on you over time. A slow shift can lull you into complacency, maybe blinding you to the gradual erosion of your own integrity. Or, if you see it coming, it can make you leap, even if a bit too quickly. Just as the frog could sense a change in temperature, our conscience whispers when our values are compromised or being challenged. Your body might also give you subtle signals. For example, my stomach often churns after certain meetings or conversations. It is telling me something. Whether it is your conscience or your tummy, it calls you to question, to leap, and to reclaim your authenticity before it's too late. Staying true to ourselves is not about seeking a comfortable existence; it's about choosing a life that aligns with our values, a life that enables us to thrive—not just survive.

Building a Healthy Culture

In my role as a chief human resources officer, I have had many experiences when behaviors did not align to company values. When that is clear, we take appropriate action. At times, we are not informed of the bad behaviors because "everyone does that so it must be acceptable here." Or when we decide to take necessary action, we might hear "but my boss did the same thing! Why am I being punished?" Situations like this cause me to worry. What is the temperature in those departments? What don't I know? How can we address issues that we cannot see directly? How can we gauge the temperature? It takes all of us. Holding ourselves, each other, and our teams accountable to our values and practices is a must for a thriving, healthy company.

A healthy culture is developed and maintained by every action and decision we make—day by day. The impact of bad behaviors and the subsequent erosion of trust is more meaningful when it's displayed by senior level leaders. You will see this reflected as their leadership shadow, which I talk about in Chapter 6.

Reflection: Leading with Your Values

In order to make decisions based on your values, you first have to know what they are, of course. You can leverage your Goldilocks framework to help guide you with this reflection. Ask yourself these questions, and answer honestly.

- Are your values clear to you?
- What would others say are your values based on your behaviors and actions? Are they clear? Does it match what you think your values are?
- Would you select your next company and/or role by digging into the culture and value tenets they subscribe to?
- Are you sure that they walk the talk?
- What values, if breached, would make you leave a company or even a relationship?

Writing a Purpose Statement

Funny enough, I wrote down my values from a work expectation but not from a life expectation when I created my original Goldilocks framework. It wasn't until I wrote down my purpose statement that I realized that my values came to life.

(continued)

The Frog in Boiling Water

(continued)

The beginning of my purpose statement is *"I need to leave the world better than I found it. To be kind."*

I also want to be with people who are kind and want to make the world around them better. To be a part of that community energizes me and gives me joy. As a result, I have left organizations and leaders whom I felt were not inherently kind. I took my leap.

Quick Takeaways: Moral Lessons

Remember these lessons from the fable of the frog in the boiling water:

- *Be tuned into your values and goals. Gradual change can be imperceptible and dangerous:* You may not realize the negative consequences of small, incremental changes until it's too late.

- *Comfort can become complacency:* The frog's initial comfort with the warmth led to his inability to react when the danger became real.

- *Awareness and vigilance are crucial:* You must be mindful of your surroundings and the changes happening around you, even if they seem insignificant.

- *It's important to be proactive and take action when needed:* The frog's inaction could have ultimately led to his demise.

Remember, leaping lily pads does not always mean leaving your company or moving away from all of your friends. The leap could be to a new project, leaping to a new idea, making the commitment to modify the pad you are on or even leaping to a new team. The point is to tap into your readiness and need for change. How will you know when to leap? This is where your Goldilocks framework comes into play. Know yourself and your values first. Then you can better evaluate to see the if and the when to find that next shiny new lily pad.

In Summary: Knowing When to Leap

I ultimately took the leap and "lived happily ever after." Whew! Unfortunately, not everyone makes the best choice. Some stay on their pad and don't realize the danger of their environment. Consider the employees or leaders at Enron or Theranos. What did they observe and what behaviors did they accept? They may have sacrificed a value or two for other rewards, like money, job security, or perhaps prestige. Those choices may have affected their personal or professional brands.

You get to decide your values and when you need to leap. Your choices will either reinforce the brand you want or erode it if they are in conflict with your values. With that in mind, here are a few things to remember before you leave this chapter:

- *Gaining clarity of your values is critical!* Do your Goldilocks exercise. Test your comments with someone who knows you well and whom you trust. Do you model those values?

- *Reflect: Are you comfortable in your surroundings or are you complacent? Can you push the change that you need?* Like that potential promotion or bonus payout, the frog's initial comfort with the warmth led to his inability to initially react when the danger became real. Don't be swayed into staying with a bad culture while waiting for that career goal. Maybe push to change the behaviors that are not acceptable around you. That next gig, new project, team, or promo is right around the corner, all with a company that lives your values.

- *You are the company you keep:* The frog's inaction and hanging out with that farmer could have ultimately led to his demise. Although I believe every experience is a learning moment, staying in a toxic culture too long, or holding onto something that is clearly going to fail, will taint your reputation if you are not careful.

I remember my mom used to say that I would be judged by the company that I kept. At first, I didn't believe her. She said this when I was in middle school and hanging out with kids who got into trouble at school. She believed that I would be guilty by association and/or I would see their behavior as acceptable behavior. Both outcomes would not be good in her book! On reflection, feedback received from my teachers and after a few conversations with my mom, I agreed and modified my peer group. I ended up with a peer group that had the same values as me. Afterwards, I felt happier. It was also the beginning of a true sense of belonging.

Be mindful that changes are usually subtle. Therefore, I love having a compass and a mirror so I can be truthful to myself when in doubt. I need to reflect often and listen intently for signals. You need that as well. Leverage your close working relationships to help gauge events—to see if they see what you are seeing. Calibrate those shifts against your values. When your body gives you signals that something is off, listen. And conversely, when it feels right and there are many proof points, you get to do your best work with passion. Become fearless. Follow your values and work on being authentic. Chapter 9 dives more into what it means to be your authentic self. Hint: Living your values is part of that authenticity!

So, what are you waiting for?

Mulan

Pursuing Authenticity

*O*nce upon a time, in ancient China, a young girl named Mulan faced a heartbreaking dilemma. The Huns threatened her empire, and an edict demanded one man from each family join the army. Her aging father, Fa Zhou, longed to serve but was too frail. A fire *burned within Mulan: a mix of filial piety and a yearning for adventure. So, under the cloak of night, she made a daring choice. With her hair cut short and her heart resolute, she disguised herself as a man and took her father's place in the ranks.*

Military training was brutal, sweat soaking through her disguised face as she struggled to keep up with the other recruits. But Mulan possessed strength she hadn't known, an inner warrior fueled by love for her family and loyalty to her country. Alongside the stern Captain Li Shang, she honed her skills, her secret simmering beneath the surface.

In the heat of battle, the Hun onslaught unleashed chaos. Mulan, her true self finally ablaze, leaped into the fray with breathtaking courage. She devised a clever strategy, outsmarting the enemy and saving Captain Li Shang's life in the process. But victory came at a cost—her secret tumbled out, shattering the fragile trust she had built with her peers. Shame threatened to consume her, but Li Shang, recognizing her valor, shielded her from dishonor.

Returning home ostracized but resolute, Mulan found solace in her family's embrace. Yet, the embers of heroism hadn't extinguished. When the Huns returned, whispering fear across the land, it was Mulan who rose again, drawing on her hard-won skills and battlefield knowledge. This time, not in the shadows, but as a beacon of hope for her people—clearly breaking the stereotype for women at that time.

151

Mulan

Leading a daring raid with Li Shang by her side, Mulan outsmarted the Hun leader, Shan Yu, and secured a resounding victory that echoed through the mountains. She returned a hero, hailed for her courage and intellect. The emperor himself knelt before her, bowing to the warrior who defied tradition and saved his empire.

Fifteen Hundred Years of Mulan!

The story of Mulan's courage, facing stereotypes, her loyalty, and the eventual emergence as her authentic self is inspiring. No wonder this folktale has been told for more than 1,500 years! Due to its longevity, I was curious about this folktale's origin. How did it survive the test of time?

I did a bit of research and learned the following:

- *Like most folktales, it started as an oral tradition:* It started as "The Ballad of Mulan," composed during the Northern Wei Dynasty (386–535 AD). Mulan's story continued to evolve and adapt over time as it was passed down through generations. Some historians suggest a warrior woman named Zhou Qing might have served as inspiration. She must have been impressive!

- *Then came the written records:* The earliest written record of her story dates back to the twelfth century, preserved in Chinese anthologies. Over the centuries, various literary adaptations further popularized and amplified the legend.

- *And finally, the story was retold in movies:* From Disney's animated films to various live-action versions, the legend of Mulan endures. The moral of her story carries onward.

A Journey to Authenticity

The key moral lesson for me is Mulan's journey toward authenticity. Mulan willingly sacrificed her comfort and identity due to the ideals of her time. Those ideals were a real constraint of the time for women. However, Mulan made that sacrifice in pursuit of her values—but it came at a cost. Eventually, Mulan's true identity emerged. Although she was originally ostracized on being disclosed as a woman, she eventually was accepted for her true feminine self and that she was needed for her strength and courage. The country put aside their societal beliefs, those false constraints, and realized they needed Mulan. They needed her strength, creativity, and courage. It no longer mattered that she was a girl—what mattered was what she could do.

When to Disclose or When to Hide?

This question has been posed to me on several occasions in my career. More times than I can count, actually. In fact, I have asked this question regarding my own disability and that of my daughter. Although our society has evolved in many ways, there remain biases threaded throughout every culture. In our example, being considered disabled or neurodiverse is typically seen as a negative. As less than. A challenge. Did you know that according to the Bureau of Labor Statistics (www.bls.gov/news.release/ pdf/disabl.pdf) about 78% of people with disabilities are either unemployed or underemployed? Just think about the loss of their magic in the world by not giving them opportunities to contribute in their unique way.

I wish I could change that narrative. In the last 12 months, I've had a father and son both approach me to seek guidance on how to navigate their attention deficit hyperactivity disorder. What do they tell managers, teachers, family, or friends? How can they show up authentically and openly without creating a negative bias on their capabilities? The son was just launching his career. He worried that his perceived "constraint" would inhibit his ability to dream big. Like Mulan, they each held superpowers. The dad was excited to get diagnosed at the same time as his son. He recognized similar attributes in himself and decided to see what the results would be. This self-awareness would also give him a better advantage to help guide his young adult son. The level of love between these two was special to see.

Meet Jules—the dad. I was fortunate to work with Jules once upon a time. He is an amazing empathetic executive leader. He leads large account management or customer success organizations. His team loves him. His energy is infectious, and he thinks creatively. Jules took his unique challenges and navigated his career successfully, but there were significant complications along the way. His hope was that his son would figure out a smoother path to success and confidence. That is when he introduced me to his son, Tiger. Wow—what a humble, smart, and caring young man!

So, we talked. Having a processing challenge or attention deficit challenge does not affect one's IQ. How you navigate the world with these challenges provides and builds strengths. We explored Tiger's strengths. What was his passion? (Yes, I gave him his Goldilocks homework, too.) With his self-awareness, humility, grit to be successful, and his confidence to be who he is openly, he will help shape the world around him to be more accepting of everyone who processes the world a little bit differently than most.

Like most people I've encountered who ask this very same question, I've been humbled by their combined spirit, openness to be authentically themselves, and eagerness to live up to their full potential. Can you imagine if we tapped into or unlocked the potential in the remaining 80% of that diverse population? The world would be even more beautiful than it is today.

Covering

"The real difficulty is to overcome how you think about yourself."

—Maya Angelou

Many people today, and perhaps even you, do not feel comfortable being your true self—either at home or work. To be authentic in life, to pursue your purpose takes courage, belief in yourself, and trust. What I've learned throughout my life is that we all hide parts or a significant amount of who we truly are. Why do we do this?

As I dug into the concept of belonging a few years ago, I learned about *covering* from Kenji Yoshino, a prominent legal scholar and the Chief Justice Earl Warren Professor of Constitutional Law at New York University School of Law.[1] He shed light on this phenomenon and its impact on us and how we show up.

Kenji is recognized for his expertise in these areas:

- *Constitutional law:* His research and writings delve into various aspects of constitutional law, including anti-discrimination law, civil and human rights, and law and literature.

- *Identity and diversity:* He actively explores the legal and social implications of identity, focusing on areas like race, gender, and sexuality. His book *Covering: The Hidden Assault on Our Civil Rights* dives into the concept of "covering" to navigate discrimination.

So, what is covering? When I read his work, it instantly clicked for me. Covering is when you hide parts of yourself or pretend to be something you are not. People do this for various reasons. However, the cost of covering is high. It takes the brain a lot of energy to maintain that cover. Energy that people could spend learning new things, creating new pieces of art, or just enjoying a moment fully without distraction.

When and Why Do We Cover Part of Ourselves?

Here are some scenarios in which you cover part of who you are:

- *Emotional covering:* This refers to the tendency to mask your true emotions, presenting a neutral or even cheerful facade while suppressing deeper feelings like sadness, anger, or vulnerability. This might be done to avoid conflict, protect yourself from judgment, or simply fit in with social expectations.

- *It's situational—selective self-disclosure:* You naturally reveal different aspects of ourselves to different people. You might share your professional ambitions with colleagues, your creative side with close friends, and your deepest fears only with a trusted loved one.

- *Socially unacceptable aspects:* Fear is a big motivator to cover. You cover parts of yourself that you deem unacceptable or undesirable in certain social contexts. Mulan hid her gender so that she could join the army in the place of her aging father. This could also involve suppressing aspects of your personality, interests, or beliefs that you fear might be met with disapproval or rejection, or even potentially put you in harm's way. For me, I hid my dyslexia, fearing it would put my career goals in jeopardy.

For whatever reason you might have, you cover a part of who you are, depending on your environment, your experiences, and your level of psychological safety. Psychological safety is important in our personal and work lives. Like many of you, I have not always experienced psychological safety in my environment. Some of my covering came from my own insecurities. I did not like aspects of myself—either how I looked (my skinny legs!), my poor spelling skills, or how I struggled to learn. When those thoughts rise up, I am less than what I could be, and I become less happy.

What Is Psychological Safety Anyway?

When you feel safe, you believe that you will not be punished or humiliated for speaking up about ideas, raising questions, concerns, or making mistakes. You feel safe to be authentically you in how you dress and perhaps even how you style your hair. It's about your personal choice. Not about what others think.

Having psychological safety is a crucial aspect of team dynamics and organizational culture because it fosters open

157

Mulan

communication, collaboration, and innovation. Teams with high psychological safety perform better and are more successful in achieving their goals. Therefore, it is essential for leaders to create an environment where team members feel safe to express themselves without fear of negative consequences.

Like I said, I do not always feel safe. It affects how I show up. It makes the day seem very long and harder than it needs to be. And at times, I am lonely. For various reasons, I've covered parts of myself throughout my life. Thankfully, I find that I cover less as I've aged. In fact, I love who I am and who I am becoming. I guess getting older gives me more perspective on life, accepting who I am without worrying about others' opinions. Another side benefit—being me also takes way less energy! And it's more fun.

But this evolution to being authentically me was a journey! If you were to look at my school photos throughout high school and college, you will notice that I changed my look to mirror those traits of my peer group. And trust me, some of those looks were awful! You can see the different styles of clothes and bad hairstyles. (I had a perm for way too long!) Maybe I was trying to find out who I was by trying on what others were doing? My "just right fit"? But more likely, I wanted to fit in and be liked.

As I entered the workforce, the covering continued. At work in my twenties and early thirties, I would wear suits and heels, style my hair like my peers, and put on makeup. I felt that I needed to "look" the part of a professional. Perhaps to be taken more seriously. And as you know, I also hid my dyslexia during that period.

I have evolved. I found my courage along the way. Like Mulan. (Well, maybe I didn't beat down the Huns and save a country, but I did emerge as my authentic self!) If you know me now, my authentic style elements are sneakers, jeans, a comfortable shirt or sweater, a natural hair style, maybe a bit of pink highlights for fun, and I wear little to no makeup!

Today, I am very open about my dyslexia and about being an introvert—seeing both as superpowers. I am a bit quirky. I'm proud to be a grandma! I continue to color my hair pink whenever the mood strikes. And best of all, I continue to learn and evolve. I'm excited to see what I will be like at age 80!

My Story: Authenticity > Superpower

As a new mom, introverted and still hiding my dyslexia while striving to build my career, I was anything but my true authentic self. As I mentioned, I wore business suits, wore makeup, modeled the behavior of those around me, and worked hard to showcase my skills. It was the challenge (and blessing) of being a new mom that broke down my walls.

There were many micro moments that led to me uncovering because striving to have it all together was exhausting. A funny memory was when my second son was born, and I just returned to work. My boys are 14 months apart—basically it felt like I had twins. I didn't know what sleep was! One day I was so tired, I went to work with baby spit up dribbled down the back of that business suit jacket and forgot to rinse the conditioner out of my hair that morning! I was too tired to notice.

(continued)

(continued)

No one said a word at work if they noticed how messy I was—they were just really nice to me that day! When I went into the restroom late that morning and saw what a mess I was, I just had to laugh. If I didn't laugh, I think I would have cried. When I finally emerged, a bit more cleaned up, I thanked my coworkers for having my back—we all laughed. It was then I shared more about my family and in return I learned more about theirs. Everyone had a story to share.

I found that sharing my typical life ups and downs and asking about my coworkers' helped me connect with them. I also became more me. I became less worried about the persona I wanted to project. I focused on just being the best me.

The World Needs Diversity—It Needs YOU

Eventually, through these messy moments of life, I found that the world was a bit more flexible. There was room for someone just like me. There is room for uniqueness. There is room for someone just like YOU. Our differences make the world a better place—a more beautiful place. Who wants to be in a room with everyone dressed the same? Acting the same? Saying the same things? We would not have innovated, survived, or evolved without unique thoughts and genetics. Those anomalies, if you will, make us stronger. Diversity of thought makes us smarter. This mixture of unique traits are why we have survived and thrived for thousands of years.

Think about it. If I knew exactly what my manager and peers would say in a critical meeting, I would just prepare enough to get the result I desired. I wouldn't stretch. But what if I didn't know their thoughts? What if they all came from different backgrounds, perspectives, and styles? What would I do? Well, if I desired a certain outcome, I would have to research more. I would seek to understand their points of view in advance of that meeting (Remember the Elephant?). I would have to dig deeper, learn more, and anticipate a whole host of questions so that when questioned, I was prepared.

That journey of getting ready for that meeting, anticipating the unknown, basically striving to touch the whole elephant, made me smarter. I gained more insights and perhaps maybe changed my hypothesis a bit based on that research. So, you see, working with and surrounding yourself with different types of people can only make you stronger and smarter. We learn from each other. I love that.

Reflection: Embracing Authenticity

People can spot phoniness a mile away. You can see it in others. When you see someone as their true authentic self, you naturally trust that person more. That authentic person also seems happier, more confident. The goal is to harness that for yourself.

Let's now dive a bit deeper into embracing YOUR authentic self.

- *Covering*: Have you ever felt like that fish that didn't quite fit in? Or perhaps more the ugly duckling? What parts of you are you covering?

(continued)

(continued)

- What was the right path for you? Was it the expected path as outlined by your parents or teachers?
- Did you model yourself based on others? Or did you find that the world is perhaps a bit more flexible so that you could carve out your own path?

- *Embracing what makes us different:* The exposure to diversity of thoughts, experiences, and passions ignited a passion in me to strive to make things better. To help others. If we all lock arms by leaning into both what we have in common with each other as well as—and maybe especially—what makes us different, we will all benefit.

  - What about you? What do you see in yourself that is unique? Do those differences make you uncomfortable? If so, have you asked yourself why?
  - Maybe if you changed your perspective and asked yourself, "What can I learn from that different point of view?" It doesn't mean you have to change your point of view. In fact, that additional insight just might make you more confident.
  - How have you embraced the unique contributions and strengths of those around you?

In Summary: Embracing Your Leadership Competencies

The story of Mulan offers valuable leadership lessons that transcend the boundaries of gender and culture. Mulan—an amazingly strong woman, especially for her time—exemplifies the qualities of an exceptional leader, demonstrating resilience, strategic thinking, agility in decision-making, and a deep sense of loyalty. Who wouldn't want to work for a leader with those fantastic traits? Let's dive a bit deeper to learn more about what set Mulan apart and why she is remembered 1,500 years later!

- *Courage to challenge stereotypes:* Mulan's journey begins with her defiance of societal expectations, boldly taking her father's place in the army despite the inherent risks and social disapproval. Her courage helped her make a big decision, but at the initial cost of her authenticity. Eventually, she emerges as her true self and is celebrated for her courage and strength.

- *Inclusion:* Embracing others' authentic selves creates belonging. She recognized the strengths and contributions of each individual, fostering a sense of unity and respect among her fellow soldiers. Because she did this, when she emerged as female, her community ended up accepting her.

- *Agile leadership:* In the face of military challenges, Mulan demonstrated her strategic prowess by devising clever plans and adapting to unforeseen circumstances. She recognized her own strengths and weaknesses, effectively using her skills to overcome obstacles and protect her comrades. She never gave up. Mulan also prioritized the safety and well-being of others, putting her own desires aside for the greater good.

I admit that I've read the folktale and watched the movie *Mulan* several times. Each time, I take away a new moral lesson that can be applied to various aspects of my life. Her courage to push on stereotypes, strategic thinking, loyalty to family, authenticity, and her leadership style serve as an inspiration to me as I seek to make a positive impact on the world. She is a badass!

Mulan also reminds me to let my team know about their own unique superpowers and how they contribute to the overall success of the team. Everyone contributes something unique to the team and thereby makes the whole team stronger. But many times, they are not aware of their impact. It is important to celebrate each person and perhaps show how they can also learn from their peers.

One day, after a long team meeting and reviewing our quarterly results, I went around the room and highlighted the unique value each of my team members brought to the table. One was an optimist—enabling all of us to dream bolder dreams. One was a pessimist—looking at the weak links and keeping us thinking pragmatically. Another one was all about the data—can the data back up our decisions? Does the data show a different path? What a great asset to have on any team! Well, you get the point. Together these amazing, unique individuals created a high-performing team. Their authentic styles and approach combined to make us all stronger.

If you have not shared an exercise like this with your team, I highly suggest you do. Each person on my team walked away feeling seen, valued, and energized. It was an emotionally charged, beautiful moment.

What's Next: A Note from Pat on Taking Action

Once upon a time, I decided to take a journey and invest in myself—personally and professionally. The stories and insights shared in this book came from that journey—a combination of my lived experiences, plus wisdom and research shared by others. I've embraced being perfectly imperfect and have pursued with gusto being my best version as I've aged. That is my personal quest.

Along my journey, I have treated my mistakes as learning moments—to be celebrated as a reflection of growth. By leveraging the wisdom embedded in this book, learning from the moral lessons within the fables and folktales, I believe I am a better me—at home, in my community, and at work. I know that I'm not alone on this journey. Goldilocks helps me knock that imposter off my shoulder, the crow reminds me to be creative and embrace challenges, the elephant taught me to broaden my perspective, the frog reminds me to follow my values, and finally Mulan inspires me with her authenticity.

They and others are now a part of your journey. You are right there with me on a quest of your own! Whether you read the chapters in sequence, jumped around, or even skipped a couple, my objective was to get you engaged, inspired, and ready to go to face your next chapter of your life's journey—wherever that adventure takes you.

It is normal to not know which path to take. Therefore, if you are noodling on possible paths, you may need a bit more time, tools to prompt you, and space for reflection. Try things out like Goldilocks to discover your just right fit. Or, like the emperor, you may need to gather more feedback to truly know the best path forward.

If you need more time and assistance, I invite you to explore the next chapter—your personal working guide. This guide section is a compilation of the lessons and tools I've shared in the prior chapters. The friends you have met in each story will continue to guide you. This is the magical part where you get to focus on you in order to unlock your story—your potential.

I look forward to hearing your stories and learning from your experiences. May the guide help you define your quest, bring your courage, and help you launch your journey with passion and curiosity. As my Irish Nanny would say—right before an adventure:

May you have the hindsight to know where you've been,
The foresight to know where you are going,
And the insight to know when you have gone too far.
(or maybe not far enough!)

Figuring out your authentic self, being comfortable and happy with who you are, is a key element I believe for life's success. This self-discovery will open up unlimited doors of opportunity in your life. I must thank Nanny for being such a good role model. Her zest for life, the ability to teach and inspire with stories and her love for others has been a guiding light in my life.

With gratitude,

Note

1. Kenji is the author of three books: *Covering: The Hidden Assault on Our Civil Rights* (Random House, 2007); *A Thousand Times More Fair: What Shakespeare's Plays Teach Us About Justice* (Ecco, 2011); and *Speak Now: Marriage Equality on Trial* (Crown, 2015).

Working Guide: Tools and Tips to Map Your Journey

"Twenty years from now you will be more disappointed by the things that you didn't do than by the ones you did do. So throw off the bowlines, sail away from safe harbor, catch the trade winds in your sails. Explore, Dream, Discover."

—Mark Twain

Embarking on Your Leadership Quest: Unlock Your Story!

Just like any epic adventure, your leadership journey thrives on your active participation and the courage to "sail away from a safe harbor"! To support you on that journey, this guide is a compilation of lessons and wisdom shared in the book. It's meant to provide you with the keys to a successful quest. Within this guide are core elements to your treasure map:

- *Simple reminders:* Refreshing insights to keep you focused on the journey ahead

- *Reflective prompts:* Questions to spark self-discovery and inspire you to act

- *Frameworks:* Tools to build your unique story and milestones to keep you on task

Dig deep. As you embark on self-reflection, remember—your story is yours alone. It's a captivating tale already in progress, written in the pages of your experiences. But the next chapters are yet to be penned. The choices you make and the questions you ask—they shape the narrative of your legacy. What lessons will you learn? What wisdom will you impart to empower others?

The key is to embrace the journey:

- *Shed your inhibitions:* Let go of limiting beliefs. Touch the vastness of your potential. Like the elephant from the fable, you are more than what others perceive they see.

- *Own your shadow:* Embrace your complexities, seek feedback, and chart the course of who you want to be.

- *Live authentically:* Live by your personal score-card—a life true to your values and goals.

- *Commit to yourself:* Honesty and vulnerability are the keys that unlock powerful outcomes. There are no wrong answers, just a chance to learn and grow. Make these promises to yourself:

  - **Truth and vulnerability:** I will be honest about my thoughts and feelings during this exploration.

  - **Attentiveness:** I will be fully present, open-minded, and ready to delve into this work. This is a continuous journey, so I'll take breaks and revisit with fresh eyes.

  - **Accountability:** I will hold myself responsible for the goals and commitments I set.

  - **Add your own commitments:**

  _____

  _____

  _____

  _____

Breaking Through What Holds You Back

What false constraints have held you back? Are there negative thoughts, limiting beliefs, or societal norms hindering your progress? Maybe it's time to silence the imposter whispering in your ear, or brush off the imposter sitting on your shoulder, where mine so often sits.

In the following space, list the self-imposed limitations that have hindered your goals. Face the constraints that you carry with you and those that others try to impose on you:

False constraint: _____

False constraint: _____

False constraint: _____

False constraint: _____

False constraint: _____

Remember: There are no bad ideas, only roadblocks waiting to be overcome. You can tackle those constraints like the Crow and propel toward your ultimate leadership potential!

Identifying Your Trust/ Accountability Partners

Next, start to visualize your ideal support system as you chase your ambitions. This might include a coach, therapist, a personal board of directors, or trusted friends and mentors. Trust and respect are key. These individuals become your accountability partners—they will check in periodically and always speak the truth to you. Think about the emperor and the value of honest feedback.

Pick at least two people who will share your journey through this exercise. Consider your current connections—who can you rely on to hold you accountable? You might have different partners for different scenarios. You get to choose. Start your list here:

Name	Relationship	Role
		Will sit down with me to review my Goldilocks and offer input
		Will nudge me on my values/ commitments
		Sees me when I falter and encourages me to be courageous

Unlocking Your Potential: A Guide to Self-Discovery and Growth

"It is not the destination, but the journey, that matters."

—T. S. Eliot.

Are you ready to embark on your leadership journey? This section of the guide equips you with powerful tools for self-discovery and growth. Begin to "own your shadow," see what drives you and the special skills you offer the world, and then chart the course on your journey to becoming the best version of you. The following three steps are meant to kick start YOU.

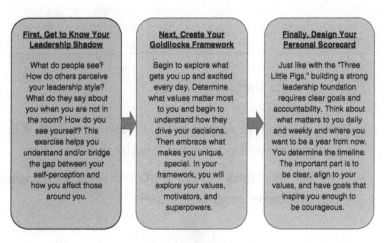

First, Get to Know Your Leadership Shadow

What do people see? How do others perceive your leadership style? What do they say about you when you are not in the room? How do you see yourself? This exercise helps you understand and/or bridge the gap between your self-perception and how you affect those around you.

Next, Create Your Goldilocks Framework

Begin to explore what gets you up and excited every day. Determine what values matter most to you and begin to understand how they drive your decisions. Then embrace what makes you unique, special. In your framework, you will explore your values, motivators, and superpowers.

Finally, Design Your Personal Scorecard

Just like with the "Three Little Pigs," building a strong leadership foundation requires clear goals and accountability. Think about what matters to you daily and weekly and where you want to be a year from now. You determine the timeline. The important part is to be clear, align to your values, and have goals that inspire you enough to be courageous.

Working Guide: Tools and Tips to Map Your Journey

Now put those steps into action. This is your journey to own! The following sections take a deeper dive along with tools to help you navigate your path, unlock your leadership potential, and become the best version of yourself.

Step 1: Get to Know Your Leadership Shadow

Imagine yourself standing in the spotlight. Depending on the angle of the light, different aspects of you are revealed. How do people perceive you as a leader? Consider how your family, friends, colleagues, and community experience your leadership in various situations.

Although your style might adapt to different settings, there will likely be recurring themes. This exercise encourages you to reflect on your leadership style and how it's perceived by others.

Start by identifying the people you interact with regularly:

Family and friends	Community members	Coworkers

Next, consider these questions:

- How do you perceive yourself as a leader? What adjectives describe your leadership style?

- How do you think others perceive your leadership? What adjectives might they use?

Honest feedback is essential. Ask trusted individuals to describe how you lead, how you treat them in your interactions, and how you make them feel. What behaviors do they wish you would do more or less of? Listen openly and be receptive to learning.

Mind the Gap!

There's often a gap between how we see ourselves versus how others see us. This exercise helps you identify that gap. Where do your views and others' views overlap? Where do they differ?

The goal is to determine if you want to adjust your leadership behaviors to better align with your ideal and how others perceive you. Remember, gaps are normal. The key is to understand the gap, how often it appears, and whether you are motivated to modify certain behaviors.

Note: You are not meant to meet everyone's expectations, but it is key to know if you are incongruent with the behaviors and attributes you want to model. You decide who you are and what makes you proud of you.

By reflecting on your leadership shadow, you can make conscious choices to become the leader you aspire to be.

Take action today! Start by reflecting on your leadership shadow—use the feedback you have gathered and the attributes of your shadow. What surprised you? What resonated most? Capture your insights here:

Attributes described by friends	Attributes described by family	Attributes described by coworkers/team

Top three attributes that surprised you most:

- _____
- _____
- _____

Top attributes and/or behaviors you want to work on:

- _____
- _____
- _____

Step 2: Create Your Goldilocks Framework

Know thyself! This section is your launching pad for defining goals by reflecting on your core values, what motivates you, your unique strengths (your superpowers), and your areas for growth to find the perfect balance for YOU.

Before diving into goals, clarity is key. Understanding your values, motivators, and aspirations equips you to, as I like to say, "chase the right rabbit." In other words, you'll be setting goals aligned with what truly matters to you. The following sections contain helpful reminders to guide you through this exercise.

Values

Values are your core principles, the things that truly matter in your life. They guide your behavior and decision-making, acting as your guiding light. They evolve with experience and define what's important to you. Do you know what would make you leap to a new lily pad? Or when you are motivated to perhaps reshape the lily pad you are on?

Your values:	List what truly matters to you?

Your values (along with the rest of your Goldilocks) serve as your compass. Your compass represents your core principles, the overall direction you want to travel in life. Like a compass pointing north, your values are constant and influence your long-term goals.

Motivators

These are the driving forces behind your actions, answering the why. Motivators are influenced by your values but can also be temporary or specific. It's easy to confuse the two during reflection.

Your motivators:	List what drives you to take action?

Motivators serve as the wind. The wind can push you in a certain direction, helping you reach your destination faster. However, the wind can change, just like motivators can be influenced by external circumstances or short-term desires. They provide the immediate push to take action.

> Values and motivators are the fuel for achieving your goals. Ideally, they'll be in sync, leading to a sense of purpose and fulfillment.

Superpowers (Your Unique Strengths and Skills)

Your superpowers are your strengths; they are the sunshine in your positive shadow. They're what others rely on and what will propel you toward your long-term goals. When you explore your shadow, these are the common themes that the people around you share as being your "secret sauce"—uniquely you. This includes the following:

- *Things you excel at and enjoy:* These are your natural talents and behaviors that bring you satisfaction and others compliment you on. You tend to lean most heavily on these skills or behaviors.

- *Essential skills, even if you don't love them:* These are the competencies you've developed that might not be your passion, but they're necessary for success. Think of them as stepping stones to future goals.

Superpowers (strengths and skills):	List what are you great at (and enjoy)? What skills are essential (even if not your passion)?

- *Emerging skills:* These are skills you have been building in the last year or so. Indicate if you enjoy practicing that skill, or again, if it is a necessary evil to get you to your next destination.

Working Guide: Tools and Tips to Map Your Journey

Emerging skills:	List what new skills or knowledge are you actively developing or learning right now?

_____

_____

_____

- *Desired skills:* List as many skills/experiences you think you want to explore (such as live/work in a different country for a year). Also, be mindful of those items that you believe are necessary but are not enjoyable. Brainstorm here!

Desired skills:	List what new skills or competencies do you believe will be increasingly valuable in the coming years?

_____

_____

_____

_____

- *Current role/life situation:* Outline what you have going on right now and indicate what gives you joy and what does not. Be as honest as you can. Perhaps weigh the various elements or rank them. That perspective will drive clarity.

Current role/life situation:	List what are you working on right now?

This is why I love the Goldilocks framework! It's a powerful tool for reflecting on the alignment with your values, motivators, and superpowers.

Keep in mind that the Goldilocks framework is a living document that evolves with you. Review and update it as you experience life changes, gain new perspectives and skills, or reach milestones. Sometimes a quick refresh is all you need; other times a deeper reflection is required to identify your next steps. I revisit mine at the end of each year or when a major change occurs in my life.

Taking time for this introspection can unlock a clearer, healthier path to your future.

Bringing Goldilocks to Life: A Sample Framework/Template

The format you choose for your Goldilocks framework is entirely up to you. Some people prefer spreadsheets, others favor PowerPoint slides or written documents. The key is the self-reflection process—being true to you.

Here's one way my friend Gloria approached this exercise that I have seen others model. Again, it is less about the framework, and more about the reflection and the clarity.

Values	Motivators (life and work)	Superpowers	Emerging skills/ learning new experiences	Desired future skills, goals, and experiences	Current job/ life scenario
Do the right thing	Always be able to pass the "red face test." Walk away from experiences that don't align.	Bringing out the best in people/empathy	AI everywhere, with a focus on generative AI. Learn and apply, then learn and apply.	Applied AI thought leader	Newly "retired" and defining my next chapter
Make the world a better place	Leave things better than I found them for the next generation.	Creativity with great analytical/operational skills	Public board education/certification	Board roles—public/private	Two kids in their early twenties
Family always	Nothing is more important than my husband and kids. Learned that the hard way and have regrets. Continuously prioritize family first.	Make things happen! Bring clarity, align on the North Star or a "minimum lovable product" and principles get stuff done.	Early-stage companies—board and advisory work; learn VC and PE	Serve on advisory boards where my experiences, skills, and superpowers make a differentce	Husband is my life partner and best friend and knows I need to keep working in some capacity.

Values	Motivators (life and work)	Superpowers	Emerging skills: Learning/new experiences	Desired future skills, goals, and experiences	Current job/ life scenario

Working Guide: Tools and Tips to Map Your Journey

Fill in this template and watch your Goldilocks framework guide you toward a future that aligns with your true self! You'll see additional columns for additional exploration if you desire to expand your thinking.

Step 3: Design Your Personal Scorecard

Congratulations! You've completed your Goldilocks framework. Now you can leverage it to craft your personal scorecard, a road map guided by your values, motivators, and superpowers.

Your scorecard starts with goals. These goals should be in perfect harmony with your Goldilocks framework. Remember, life is a journey, and your goals will evolve as you achieve milestones, learn, and face challenges. Your scorecard is your compass, keeping you focused and helping you to simplify decision-making.

The scorecard has two key elements—the what and the how.

The What

This defines your goals and the metrics for measuring success in each focus area. Craft SMART goals: specific, measurable, achievable, relevant, and time-bound.

Here's an example:

Category	Goals	Metrics and time frame
Financial	(e.g. save for a down payment)	($$$ saved in X months)
Health	(e.g. improve cardiovascular health)	(Reduce resting heart rate by Y points in Z months)
Career	(e.g. master a new skill)	(Become proficient in X software by Y date)
Family/ community	(e.g. volunteer for a cause I care about)	(Dedicate Z hours per month to volunteering)

Now it's your turn—what is your scorecard?

Category	Goals	Metrics and time frame

As you build your scorecard, do the following:

- *Align it with your Goldilocks framework:* Ensure your goals reflect your values and motivators.

- *Make sure it's actionable and measurable:* Can you take action and track progress toward your goals? If not, why not? Is there a false constraint in your way?

- *Personalize your categories:* This exercise is only a starting point. Choose categories that resonate with you.

The How

The how connects your actions to your values and motivators. Refer to the values you outlined in this guide. When evaluating progress, ask yourself the following:

Are my actions aligned with the values I'm committed to? If not, why not?

Remember: Your Goldilocks framework is the foundation for setting goals that matter. The scorecard helps you translate those goals into actionable steps, keeping you on track to live your best life. When evaluating progress against goals, also ask yourself if you are modeling the behaviors/values you are committed to.

Holding Yourself Accountable and Reviewing Your Personal Scorecard

It's time to take action and own your journey! Writing goals and metrics is a great first step, but staying accountable is where the magic happens. Here's how to make your scorecard a powerful tool:

- *Schedule reviews:* Set regular dates to review your scorecard—weekly, monthly, quarterly, or annually. Choose a frequency that works for you.

- *Track your progress:* Document your achievements and any setbacks. Reflect on the why behind both.

Internal or external factors can affect your progress. Identify them so you can adjust.

- *Embrace flexibility:* This is your scorecard, not a rigid script. Don't get discouraged by setbacks. See them as opportunities to adapt and make adjustments.

- *Learn and celebrate:* As your scorecard evolves, embrace victories and setbacks as opportunities for growth. Remember to embrace your growth mindset!

Now is the time! Start your quest, write your story, and refine your shadow. Lead a life brimming with purpose. Savor the journey and embrace the growth mindset discussed previously. Remember, you're not alone. We're all on unique quests, but hopefully you now feel more confident and clearer about your path.

This is your story to tell! Share your journey, your challenges, and your triumphs. Inspire others as you chase your dreams. Let others learn from your experiences. The world awaits your unique contribution!

> *"You're braver than you believe, stronger than you seem, and smarter than you think."*
> —Winnie the Pooh, A. A. Milne stories

Acknowledgments

This book is the result of a village—three amazing people whose support have made this journey both magical and fun. From providing constructive feedback on early drafts to being my dance partners throughout the process, their contributions were invaluable. Keeping the story theme in mind, I will do my best to introduce you to these three incredible human beings who danced alongside me to weave this book into your leadership narrative. Once upon a time, with Goldilocks figuratively perched on my shoulder, I encountered MaryAnne Viegelmann, Darrin Caddes, and Bryn Lewis. Our paths converged in various chapters of my career, and in a way, it felt like an instant connection was formed. Each of them has contributed to the moral of my story, aiding me in becoming a better version of myself.

Let's begin with MaryAnne Viegelmann—or as we fondly call her, MAV. Our journey spans more than 20 years, starting from my first CHRO role at Align where she began as our HR intern. Our relationship has continued to evolve across various companies since then. Her unwavering support and belief in me gave me the extra courage needed to pen this book. Her extraordinary ability to engage others, dream big, and bring order to chaos is truly invaluable! MAV played a pivotal role in uniting all parties involved, including our partnership with Wiley, to turn this dream into reality. Yet, what I cherish most is our friendship.

Now, let me introduce Darrin Caddes! Oh my goodness, he's the most creative, caring human being. I consider myself fortunate to have met Darrin during our time together at Plantronics. Our conversations always brought me joy. As a fellow dyslexic and creative artist, I'm in awe of the art he creates. When I approached him about illustrating this book, he didn't hesitate. His illustrations brought my fables and stories to life. Darrin is unique and generous in nature, and I am forever grateful that our paths crossed and our friendship grew.

Finally, Bryn Lewis! We first crossed paths at Procore, but our true connection unfolded during a stroll through Shoreline Park in Santa Barbara, California. Bonding over our shared life experiences, our Virgo tendencies, and our mutual passion to leave a lasting impact on this earth, we found common ground. (Her volunteer work at the Braille Institute teaching art with me, stands out as just one example of the positive influence she has on others.) Her encouragement, support, and roll-up-your-sleeves energy were instrumental in pushing this book across the finish line. Thank you for your friendship!

Each of these amazing individuals was brought into my life through the power and magic of Goldilocks. My journey, in search of my just right fit, hopping to new lily pads, led me to them, and I am eternally thankful.

About the Author

Pat Wadors grew up as the youngest of eight siblings. She was diagnosed with dyslexia while in college but has leaned on her neurodiversity as a strength. She is a mother to three millennials, grandmother twice, and wife of thirty years. Introvert by nature, Pat is an advocate for results over talk and works feverishly to embrace the quieter voices. A driver for writing this book is her personal purpose: "I need to leave the world better than I found it, to be kind, to give more than I get, to make a difference."

Known for transformational and strategic human resources (HR) leadership, Pat believes that organizations thrive when they have a blend of people with differing backgrounds and ways of thinking, and who feel they belong as a contributor to the company's success. As a LinkedIn learning instructor, Pat is known for her course on "Diversity, Inclusion, and Belonging," which was recognized in 2021 as a top 10 global course on LinkedIn.

Pat has held various HR leadership and chief human resources officer positions in the technology sector, including roles at UKG, Procore Technologies, ServiceNow, LinkedIn; Plantronics, Inc.; and Yahoo! She has served on the boards of several prominent technology companies, such as UKG, Second Harvest Food Bank, and El Camino

Hospital. Currently, she holds board positions at Accolade, Inc., and Moloco.

A multiple-time recipient of the National Diversity Council's Top 50 Most Powerful Women in Technology award, Pat is renowned for her transformative and strategic HR leadership. She is a sought-after speaker on diversity and inclusion topics. Pat earned a BS in business administration and a minor in psychology from Ramapo College of New Jersey.

Index